SOCIAL MEDIA AND THE ISLAMIC STATE

This book examines how social media has transformed extremist discourse. Drawing on ISIS and their sophisticated use of social media platforms and PR concepts, it explores the ways in which the outfit was able to recruit, mobilise and spread fundamentalist propaganda in regions where it had little physical presence.

One of the first studies to draw a link between international diplomacy, the rise of fundamentalism and public relations, this book will be of great interest to scholars and researchers of defence and strategic studies, especially those working on ISIS propaganda, Middle East Studies, media studies, digital humanities, communication studies, public relations and international relations, as well general readers.

Ella Minty is a PR practitioner, elected member of the CIPR council (2017–2018) and board member (2018). She is also a former UK Government Communication Service and Institute of Directors mentor, published author and university lecturer. She has almost 20 years of experience in corporate reputation, leadership and crisis management, and has also been an adviser to several governments on their national branding strategies.

'Ella Minty shows how a strategic and innovative use of social media rooted in the knowledge of history's silent forces can be a powerful tool to fight terrorism. A must-read for foreign policy strategists.'

— **Diego Gilardoni**, international communication consultant and author of *Decoding China*

'Ella Minty is the ideal communication professional to write about "Social Media and the Islamic State". Her experience and depth of knowledge on the topic are unmatched. As a public relations professional now teaching the next generation(s) of PR pros, I look forward to reading her published work and encouraging my students to read it as well and take to heart her observations.'

— **Kirk Hazlett**, APR, Fellow PRSA, Adjunct Professor, Communication, The University of Tampa; Director and Ethics Officer, Tampa Bay Chapter, Public Relations Society of America

'Ella has delved into a communications issue that should concern us all – how do we win over the hearts and minds of those who have been seduced by extremism? This is a fascinating read that should be widely read by both fellow communicators and those working in government.'

— **Alex Malouf**, EMENA Chair of the International Association of Business Communicators; Board Member of the Global Alliance for Public Relations and Communication Management; Member of the National Advisory Council, College of Communication and Media Sciences, Zayed University

'Public relations, taken seriously, has a large contribution to make to the solution of intractable social and political problems. Ella Minty takes this view of public relations into confronting challenges posed by international terrorism – and expands our understanding of these, and public relations' potential role.'

— **Jon White PhD**, Visiting Professor, Reading University Henley Business School, and Honorary Professor, Cardiff University School of Journalism, Media and Cultural Studies

'With wide and comprehensive experience in the field of public relations, Ella Minty is an evangelist, in a good way. Utterly passionate in promoting communications as a force for good in the world, she is untiring in her quest. This highly informative and very readable monograph is a valuable testament to her commitment, recommended to all with an interest in politics, communications and extremism.'

— **Jem Thomas**, Director of Training and Research, Albany Associates

'What are now recognised as industrial disciplines, "Communications" and/or "PR" have always been part of counterinsurgency (CI) and counter terrorist (CT) campaigns. Ella's work makes it clear that in the 21st century CI/CT environment, there is a greater need than ever for sovereign states and supra national actors to engage with developing best practice from industry to maintain optimum results.'

– **Paddy Blewer**, Global PR Director specialising in
government advisory and foreign direct investment services

'Ella Minty's book could not be more timely, and could not address an issue of greater importance. This is a must-read analysis from one of the PR industry's most senior and most esteemed practitioners.'

– **Francis Ingham**, Public Relations and Communications
Association Director General; Chief Executive of the
International Communications Consultancy
Organisation; LGComms Executive Director

'The rise of ISIS has painfully demonstrated that engaging communities quickly and effectively can be a matter of life and death. Ella Minty makes a compelling case for how public relations can counter this new generation of social media-savvy terrorists and be a force for good in the world.'

– **Rob Smith**, editor, *Influence*

'*Social Media and the Islamic State* is a forceful and incisive account of how the Islamic State came to dominate social media, and the inadequacy of state responses to this new challenge. Were opportunities missed to combat IS on social media itself? Minty suggests there were. In addition to the standard arsenal of surveillance and disruption, she suggests that more activist and emotionally-aware interventions, especially those crowdsourcing input from other users, might have been helpful. Her monograph is a succinct and well-focused starting point for considering how we do better in future.'

– **Alastair McCapra**, CEO, Chartered Institute
of Public Relations

SOCIAL MEDIA AND THE ISLAMIC STATE

Can Public Relations Succeed Where Conventional Diplomacy Failed?

Ella Minty

Routledge
Taylor & Francis Group

LONDON AND NEW YORK

First published 2020
by Routledge
2 Park Square, Milton Park, Abingdon, Oxon OX14 4RN

and by Routledge
52 Vanderbilt Avenue, New York, NY 10017

Routledge is an imprint of the Taylor & Francis Group, an informa business

British Library Cataloguing-in-Publication Data
A catalogue record for this book is available from the British Library

Library of Congress Cataloging-in-Publication Data
A catalog record for this book has been requested

ISBN: 978-0-367-17341-8 (hbk)
ISBN: 978-0-367-18816-0 (pbk)
ISBN: 978-0-429-19884-7 (ebk)

Typeset in Bembo
by Apex CoVantage LLC
Printed and bound by CPI Group (UK) Ltd, Croydon, CR0 4YY

CONTENTS

FOREWORD

In 2004, I spent some time in Tripoli as part of the joint US/UK team which worked with the then Libyan authorities to implement Muammar Gaddafi's decision to eliminate the country's WMD capabilities. Over dinner with our Libyan hosts, I asked a senior military officer why his leader had taken such a momentous decision. His answer was simple, without hesitation and memorable: 'the Cold War is over.'

My stay in Tripoli is as distant from today as from 1989, and yet we are still coming to terms with the end of the Cold War. Frightening though that period was with its threat of Mutually Assured Destruction, at least the enemy was a known quantity possessing the traditional qualities of statehood: a defined population, borders and a government. In hindsight, at least, the success of deterrence demonstrated that the two heavily armed powers understood each other sufficiently to navigate the ideological chasm between them and avoid the ultimate calamity.

The 'asymmetric threat' which is the subject of this book seems altogether different from those which preceded it. Whether or not it is graver is another matter. Some Western students of geopolitics argue that we should still regard traditional state adversaries as the greater danger. But, however militarily limited the so-called 'Islamic State' may be, and however statistically rare its attacks on (at least) our own countries, its monstrous ambitions, the unfamiliarity of asymmetric warfare and its ability to impinge on the daily lives of civilians without warning ensure that it commands the horrified attention of both policymakers and publics.

Terrorism, as the name implies, is about instilling fear – and unconventional warfare terrifies because it is so difficult to pin down. This is not only (or perhaps not even primarily) because of its kinetic capability but because it is in many ways about pursuing a communication – or psychological – goal. As a communication campaign, it deploys confusion to wrongfoot its adversaries: while its language and values often seem 'medieval' to the modern Western mind, its tools are often as contemporary and sophisticated as its physical weaponry.

When I attended a business briefing by a British security official, I remember being impressed and horrified in equal measure to see the smooth sophistication – dare I say the corporate banality? – of the terrorists' social media and publications. When Al-Qaeda was described as a 'franchise', it seemed like a clever metaphor, but there is no doubting the terrorists' use of up-to-date business techniques.

As Ella Minty points out eloquently in this book, social media provides a new battleground, involving an ever-larger part of the world's population, on which insurgents can compete on equal terms with incumbents or even do better. Her conclusion is that traditional stuffed-shirt diplomacy is not up to the task and must be complemented, if not replaced, by social media–savvy PR specialists who can appeal to the contemporary currency of emotion. If they can, it's undoubtedly worth the effort, as it would mean that more can be achieved to keep us safe from terrorism without recourse to military action.

If we focus on their method rather than on their murderous intent, then the Islamic State and their like are, in some ways, like any legitimate start-up or campaign group seeking to disrupt established governments and corporates. They understand the latest techniques, recruiting bright young minds, and they are not bound by legal, bureaucratic or corporate constraints from going in the most effective ways straight to their audience's heart.

Their tactics are not entirely new – for example, television was used to great effect by the combatants in the Yugoslav Wars both to enthuse potential supporters and persuade foreign governments to intervene, or not, according to the various parties' strategic aims.

Can PR play this positive role? If so, it should have a significantly beneficial effect on the standing of an occupation which, despite the efforts of this book's author and other serious practitioners, still struggles to be regarded by many as a proper 'profession'. It deserves the chance: just as the more egregious examples of 'spin' do not delegitimise democratic politics, so PR should not automatically be defined by its abuses. And just as the deployment of argument and influence are central to the law, so – when faced with opponents such as the Islamic State – democratic societies need to defend themselves in the court of public opinion.

If we are to assess the ability of PR to help, one of the challenges is to understand exactly what success means. When the Islamic State claims to act like a conventional nation, success is easy to define in terms of capturing or retaining territory. But as a wider ('terrorist') movement, its ability to impose its will either on supporters or its enemies/victims is harder to measure.

As the security agencies remind us, while they have to succeed every day in keeping us safe, the terrorists only have to succeed once. So, in this sense, some failure is inevitable. And even if absolute military victory is possible, winning over all hearts and minds is not.

But governments owe it to their voters to try. I suspect that the demise of conventional government and diplomacy may be somewhat exaggerated: nation-states and international organisations show no signs of fading away. But, just as corporates should learn from agile start-ups if they want to avoid being disrupted, it makes sense to governments to learn from those who make their living from using the latest communications platforms to appeal to their audience's hearts as well as minds.

Old dogs can certainly learn new tricks. The value of Ella Minty's thoughtful book is to bring the two worlds together, offering practical approaches to confronting one of our age's greatest challenges.

By David Landsman OBE MA PhD,
former British Charge d'Affaires in Yugoslavia,
former British ambassador to both Albania and Greece,
former head of the UK's Counter Proliferation Department

PREFACE

I've always been a great believer in the power of public relations to change the world for the better. In 2013, after the Rana Plaza disaster in Bangladesh, I joined forces with a group of peers across the world – including powerful US lobbyists – and started a concerted social media campaign to ensure that no retailer in the UK nor the US took further advantage of the squalor and poor working conditions of those less fortunate than we are and that safe and fair working conditions were provided for the Bangladeshi working for the major fashion houses and famous retailers across the world.

In the summer of 2015, ISIS was causing havoc across the Middle East, and its atrocities held the world media's headlines for many weeks. It was a new form of terrorism, one that was not afraid to use all media channels available to it to appeal to one of our most basic emotions: fear. For me, ISIS was a new and fascinating challenge – no other terrorist organisation has taken the tools and techniques of PR and strategic communication to the level of perfection, one could argue, that ISIS has.

Also, in the same summer of 2015, I got in touch with some prominent members of the PR community and asked them: 'Why don't we join our forces and start a similar campaign against ISIS? They have won, for sure, the social media "call to arms" and, if we don't do it, it's unlikely that the current diplomatic approaches will.'

My request knocked on closed doors, with one of my peers arguing that 'you can't use social media to persuade or alter opinion when the opposition is using the communication strategies of terrorism and war propaganda. . . . ISIS needs to be countered with black hat comms that would be broadly deemed unethical by most of us in this group.'

Another colleague said, 'I think the fundamental difference between your successful campaign [Rana Plaza] and a potential campaign against ISIS is stark.

The former relies on widespread approval in the West to sell products, the latter doesn't care about winning over normal folks in a democracy.'

There was, however, one colleague who could see that we, the 'PR people' can play a very well-defined role should we choose to. She said: 'You have to start somewhere, and what Ella suggests is an engagement piece that forms part of the wider plan.'

If my colleagues, whose views I quoted above, had agreed to join our forces and present a clear proposal to the UK government (and not only) on how we could support their fight against this new form of social media–savvy terrorism, this book would have never been written. We would all have been somewhere in the shadows, using our knowledge and various engagement techniques honed over decades of practice and study, doing our best to deter 'the war for the soul' that ISIS was fighting.

But my colleagues didn't agree to it. I have therefore made it my mission to write this book, and I can only hope that it will empower the academic and practice community of public relations and communication sciences to consider expanding our sphere of influence and support as an industry and, one day, as a profession.

As for the diplomatic and counterintelligence communities, I do hope that they will find this book insightful and interesting. The world has changed enormously in the last 30 years, and, today, public pressure and social activism bear a lot of influence not just on businesses but on international affairs and international relations. Those working in public relations know how to speak and relate to their publics, young and old, rich and poor, foreign and domestic, white or black.

Public relations is about public emotions, behaviours, change. Diplomacy, as recently stated by Sir Simon McDonald, the head of the UK's Foreign Office, is 'letting others have your way'. The former speaks with masses; the latter speaks with governments. If they join their forces, they will succeed in tackling the new forms of 'PR-savvy' extremism at their core.

ACKNOWLEDGEMENTS

Without my husband's unwavering support and belief in me, this book would have never been written.

Rob Smith, the editor of CIPR's *Influence*, had a significant role in my decision to write this book, as had David Landsman's PhD OBE advice.

I would also like to thank my editor, Aakash Chakrabarty, for his guidance and support.

ABBREVIATIONS

App	Application
CEO	Chief Executive Officer
CIA	Central Intelligence Agency
CSCC	Center for Strategic Counterterrorism Communications
DARPA	Defense Advanced Research Projects Agency
FCO	Foreign Commonwealth Office
FTSE	Financial Times Stock Exchange
GBP	Great Britain pound
GCC	Gulf Co-operation Council
ICSR	International Centre for the Study of Radicalisation and Political Violence
ISIS	Islamic State
IRA	Irish Republican Army
KSA	Kingdom of Saudi Arabia
MI5	The Security Service
MOD	Ministry of Defence
NATO	The North Atlantic Treaty Organization
NGO	Non-governmental organisation
NYSE	New York Stock Exchange
OECD	Organisation for Economic Co-operation and Development
PR	Public Relations
Prof	Professor
TRAC	Terrorism Research and Analysis Consortium
TV	Television
UK	United Kingdom
UN	United Nations

UNESCO	United Nations Educational, Scientific and Cultural Organization
UNSC	United Nations Security Council
USA	United States of America
USD	United States dollar

INTRODUCTION

'He appears to have followed almost exactly to a "T" the instructions that ISIS has put out in its social media channels before with instructions to their followers on how to carry out such an attack.'

John Miller, Deputy Commissioner for
Intelligence and Counterterrorism
New York Police Department (Chavez, Yan,
Levenson and Almasy 2017)

Social media has created a new frontier which is transforming the way our politics, economic affairs, security and diplomacy are conducted. More than half of the world's foreign ministries are now active on social media – but the real challenge for diplomats is not how to incorporate social media into their strategy but who and how to target, since, in the past, diplomats were expected to engage primarily with political and business elites.

The threat to controlled communications is a very direct challenge to a government's public diplomacy, and the sheer speed and openness of digital communications can stymie the carefully honed subtleties of traditional diplomacy (Cooper 2017).

Today, with instant communication and instant media attention, it's much more difficult to make backstage deals. It appears that the new age of diplomacy has more in common with the principles of chaos theory than with the subtle manoeuvring of the times gone by (Cooper 2017).

It could be that the traditional view of the diplomatic workforce must be rethought: more people who have an understanding of technology and innovation must be brought into those tradition-bound halls of power and foreign ministries around the world. Times are changing, and now there is more and more evidence that, even in this tradition-bound institution of power, social media can be used to both communicate and drive change (Cooper 2017).

However, although there are many governments around the world with a clear presence on social media, 'being there' does not necessarily mean that they have an impact, that they resonate with their various categories of stakeholders nor that they can obtain the buy-in and approval of those they are targeting.

Anyone, provided they have a reliable internet connection, can be on social media – and many are. Almost half of the world's population, according to Hootsuite's 'Digital Around the World in 2019' (Hootsuite 2019), is active on social media, with an actual figure of 3.484 billion active social media users.

The vast global scale of interactions via social media means international relations are being devolved – pursued at the individual level and privatised – and mediated by technology companies which are often perceived to be synonymous with the official United States (US) foreign policy interests. The speed and scale of these interactions can make it hard or impossible for governments to understand, respond or attempt to control events (British Foreign Policy Group 2017) as they unfold online.

Facebook, which has founded some of the world's most used social media platforms, has recently been found to have played an active part (albeit vehemently denied) in subverting the democratic processes in both the United Kingdom (UK), given its involvement with Cambridge Analytica (House of Commons 2019), as well as in the United States during President Trump's presidential election campaign.

The relative and absolute decline in profile of UK's Foreign Commonwealth Office (FCO) as a principal mediator between foreign and domestic interests poses another challenge. If all citizens are now unofficial diplomats, and private companies are curating and strongly influencing international relations, to what extent is it possible to align a credible national perspective or response on any particular issue (British Foreign Policy Group 2017)?

Harnessing the growing power of social media can support but not replace a foreign policy strategy. In order to resonate, such a strategy might consider engaging with the value- and issue-driven agendas prevalent on social media. Those soft-power assets which best promote these values and issues should be identified and sensitively supported, including their social media outreach (British Foreign Policy Group 2017).

Global internet usage continues to grow at a steady 10% per year, reaching 46% of the global population. It is fuelled by emerging markets, notably India, and based on the current adoption rates, 2026 is estimated to be the year when everyone in the world will have the ability to get online (Waddington 2017).

Information today is no longer bound by geographical or spatial boundaries, and people can even form virtual communities of their own (Pavlik 1996). The lack of physical, time-honoured boundaries and the near impossibility of curbing content online have led to the flourishing of typically censored material which, no more than half a century ago, would have been considered highly inappropriate to present on the front cover of any magazine/newspaper.

The internet has changed the way in which 21st-century governments, diplomats and people consume and use information. It is the internet, this 'electronic network of networks that links people and information through computers and other digital devices that allows person-to-person communication and information retrieval' (DiMaggio, Hargitai, Neuman and Robinson 2001:307), that has brought communities of global, transboundary interests closer.

Symbolism is an intrinsic tool for diplomats and members of international organisations – especially since diplomacy and international relations do not take lightly any form of bluntness or plain speaking. As will be illustrated throughout this book, symbolism played an immense role in ISIS' rise and in the international community's perceived and actual inability to stifle extremist symbolism.

Pomp and ceremony are engrained in traditional diplomacy – so is a measured, contained and often sombre attitude in the public and private lives of diplomats themselves. The new jihadist movements' recruitment style is at the opposite extreme – today's youth will not be swayed by discipline and overly complex engagement mechanisms but by humorous and easy to understand concepts, symbols and postulates.

The new form of terrorism displayed by ISIS has taken the international community by surprise – conventional diplomacy and warfare teach us that war needs a battlefield: ground, water or air, although lately cyberwarfare is gaining notoriety, too. The international community and national governments did not expect new wars to take place online or be streamed live – the unpredictability of and difficulty in pigeonholing ISIS and other similar terror groups is becoming increasingly difficult. They do not fit a prescribed pattern, nor do the world's mainstream or specialised universities have formal military or university courses dedicated to studying this new form of terrorist aggression underpinned by behavioural nudging.

Given the void of constructive dialogue and appropriate diplomatic channels, corroborated with conventional diplomacy's difficulty to engage in a formal dialogue with representatives of extremist factions, a power gap and power surge have simultaneously occurred: the power gap has been quickly filled by fundamentalist propaganda and indoctrination, and the closure of the power gap has led to Islamic fundamentalism gaining unprecedented reach and influence in the 21st-century globalised world.

Today, there is a lack of structured efforts from peacekeeping international organisations and multi-government structures to tackle the appeal of online extremism. The international community's efforts seem to be carried out on an individual basis, and they do not seem to be part of a wider, more inclusive and consistent counternarrative strategy. These efforts largely address the physical needs of those affected by the extremist conflicts: shelter, food and water. If the cause, not its effects, continues to be allowed to thrive, the humanitarian, cultural and social crisis in ISIS-plundered territories will hardly ever end.

The attacks in Paris and London during the past three years clearly indicate that the extremists will continue to exploit, and their narrative will be influenced by, developments in media technology, and that their masterful use of new media will continue to present national governments and the international community with difficult choices (Burke 2015:243).

The addition of participatory aspects to power-based PR for terrorists, facilitated by the social online platforms, has brought productive results for ISIS. The global threat of jihadist terrorism has grown more acute, owing mostly to the rise of ISIS – this hybrid organisation that combines elements of a proto-state, a millenarian cult, an organised crime ring and an insurgent army led by highly skilled former Baathist military and intelligence personnel.

The ultimate goal of ISIS is that of destabilising and eventually taking over Saudi Arabia – if this were to happen, the consequences not only for the region but for the entire world would be profound (Stern 2015:62).

ISIS has been able to influence its target publics and motivate them to carry out attacks in their home territories. Has the international community fully grasped the potential of social media in the fight against ISIS and Islamic fundamentalism? What messages from jihadists induce young Westerners to become involved with ISIS? What convinces young people from Europe, Australia, Canada and the United States – many of whom are technically runaways, still in their teens – to leave their homelands to join ISIS on the battlefield?

What risks does a country face when its nationals communicate and establish relationships with members of ISIS? Can the jihadist social network propaganda machine be shut down, and weighing all factors in, is stopping ISIS' rhetoric on the internet the best course of action?

ISIS' extensive online presence is coupled with the superior quality of their media production, with the planned use of soft focus, slow fades, colour saturation, superimpositions and carefully layered soundtracks. All these means and methods are intended to ensure a viral social media engagement (Ibish 2015), leaving nothing to the imagination (Kappas 2017).

If one were to remove the sinister and the sombre from ISIS' media productions, one would highly likely believe that some of the world's best advertising and PR agencies had been involved in creating such catchy, personable and resonating propaganda materials.

Rather than deploying trained forces at the target venues to carry out attacks, ISIS' social media strategy nurtures and trains followers in their home regions. This influence can be witnessed in the massacres at Bataclan Theatre in Paris (Brooking and Singer 2016), Nice, Manchester Arena, London Bridge, Westminster Bridge, Borough Market and many more.

Today, online interactions are far more important for the young generation than face-to-face ones; the 'real' world, for many young people, especially those living in emerging economies and established democracies, is online. Today, the governments' and international community's credibility is waning – people tend to believe their friends and families far more than any authorities or government representatives.

The ensuing chapter of this book – 'Literature review' – will analyse ISIS' use of social media and the internet's appeal to extremist groups. Only a selection of references in this regard is discussed in this chapter since there is a considerable amount of literature on this topic.

The 'Literature review' chapter intends to set the context for this book, contextualising the challenges posed by the extremists' use of social media to the international community.

1

LITERATURE REVIEW

Social media, as a communication and engagement medium, belongs to the wider discipline of PR. Richards (2004) classified public relations as power- and value-based, grouping the audiences as participatory and spectacle, respectively. According to him, in power-based PR, terrorists have their opposing and favouring publics to whom they communicate their messages through visible aggressive and bloody actions. On the other hand, governments retaliate against this powerful imagery by using and displaying sophisticated weaponry, ammunition and images of precision-sharp bombings.

According to Klausen (2014), the literature on terrorism is usually focused on the theatre of terrorist spectaculars which eclipses the reality: terrorists also use the internet for organising and planning, preaching and entertaining their supporters. In fact, most of the online communications of terrorists are routine to the point of appearing innocuous.

According to the United Nations Office on Drugs and Crime (2012), the internet is utilised to promote, especially for recruitment purposes, radicalisation, training, financing, planning and execution of terrorist attacks.

The post-9/11 international arena, especially the Euro-Atlantic zone, appears to give an even greater visibility to Prof Said's (2003) assertion made more than four decades ago, according to which there is no other religion or cultural group other than Islam so affirmatively and categorically described as being a threat to Western civilisation.

Relevant in this regard are the international surveys habitually run by the Pew Global Attitudes Project. One of their reports, published in 2005 and entitled 'Islamic Extremism: Common Concern for Muslim and Western Publics', was run in 17 countries and totalled 17,766 respondents. The key finding of this survey was an increased concern in the Euro-Atlantic arena related to the danger posed by Islamic extremism. Fifty-two percent of the Russian respondents, 48%

of the Indian respondents, 43% of the Spanish respondents, 35% of the German respondents, 34% of the British respondents, 32% of the French and Dutch respondents and 31% of the American respondents were 'extremely concerned with the extremism in their countries'. With the rise of ISIS and social media's grappling penetration worldwide, the percentages in the Pew survey of over a decade ago are likely to have increased significantly today.

In an article for PRWeek (2015), Peter LaMotte, currently senior vice president of Chernoff Newman, argued that 'extremists harnessing the Internet's reach to propagandize and recruit is by no means new, dating back to online forums and message boards.' In the last five years, ISIS commanded news coverage not just because of the group's media-grabbing abilities and its heightened public awareness but also because of its uncanny capacity to instil awe and fear.

According to Morozov (2012a), 'as the Internet takes on even a greater role in the politics of both authoritarian and democratic states, the pressure to forget the context will only grow.' In his book, *The Net Delusion – The Dark Side of Internet Freedom*, Morozov makes particular reference to a series of statements on the freedom of the internet made by then Secretary of State Hillary Clinton in January 2010. Mrs Clinton, in her statements, would hail the pacifist potential of the online technologies, considering the 'Freedom of Information a pillar of peace and security as well as a certain foundation for the global progress', while the author argues that the 'internet technologies contain evolutions that are not only complex but, also, contradictory.'

In a study published by Soufan Group (2015), it is argued that, paradoxical for such a media-savvy terrorist organisation, private internet use inside ISIS compounds has been banned. Starting September 2015, the group's fighters and high-ranking officials have been barred from holding personal internet accounts (both e-mail and social networks), and mobile phones are also tightly restricted.

The reason for this ISIS outside-communication ban is, one could argue, very clear: just as disenfranchised Muslims have been easy targets to attract and convert to the twisted ISIS idealism via social media and other forms of online communication, the same could prove true for any sort of government-targeted communication which may resonate with those fighters willing to give their lives for the 'caliphate's' cause – social media platforms can be, after all, dual carriage ways for communication and targeted engagement.

According to one of the many articles written by *The Economist* (2015) on the topic of ISIS, part of ISIS' means of mass communication and engagement outputs was represented by a bimonthly online magazine, radio broadcasts in five languages and video games. It appears that, at that time, the international governments' intervention to hamper and, eventually, put a stop to ISIS' global messaging was feeble because, according to a report from Brookings Institution, 'by December 2014 the Islamic State had almost 12,000 individual Twitter accounts, with 92% of these sending up to 50 different tweets daily.'

Ever since the deadly jihadist assault on the United States' facilities in Benghazi, Libya, in 2012, 'it has become even more difficult for diplomats to engage with local officials, politicians and activists who are working to foster improved governance and the protection of minority rights' (Stern 2015). The current means and methods of global dialogue and bilateral engagement – diplomatic, international and extremist – have been dramatically affected by the rise of social media.

The diplomatic communication scene has changed considerably over the last six centuries. Where, in the past, diplomatic dialogue was primarily carried out through written documents or royal and/or church emissaries, today the communication landscape is very different. The influence of means of mass communication such as television, mobile phones, social media platforms and a variety of anonymised apps have made diplomatic communication both easier and harder.

In the 21st century a new form of diplomacy and public engagement is taking shape in the world's democracies and, in some cases, in the totalitarian states – that of the common people exerting a direct influence on their government's international affairs and policies. The Arab Spring, the terrorist attacks in France in 2015 and 2016 and in the UK in 2017, the Syrian refugee crisis and, especially, the photo of Aylan Kurdi's little body (the three-year-old Syrian refugee) washed up on a Turkish beach in 2015 have shaped and continue to shape the international and national diplomatic narrative.

Social media platforms, internet availability, the anonymity of social media users and the penetration rates of internet-connectable devices have made it much easier for a special group of actors to communicate and mobilise – the extremist factions – and much harder for nation-states and government agencies to control, identify, monitor and respond to them. However, as argued by Tom Fletcher (2016), the UK's former ambassador to Lebanon, social media and 'the ability to talk directly to people is changing the nature of diplomacy and making it more open in the process.'

Furthermore, Fletcher argued that 'an army of diplomats' is needed, one which is

> using new digital tools in an authentic, engaging and purposeful way. . . . We need a permanent cadre of digital professionals who can drive digital diplomacy across the network. . . . Our content should make people lean forward.

While Mr Fletcher's argument has a lot of merit to it, one of the key questions for the members of the diplomatic corps is related to what that engagement should entail and whether governments can operate in the same way as other social media actors can.

Perhaps, while it is very clear that there are numerous government activities that do not belong and should not belong on conversationalist platforms such as social media, this should not in any way impede a constant engagement and conversation not just with those individuals who have, after all, elected those governments (in the case of democratic states) but, primarily, with those individuals who can destabilise the fabric of the state and the actual safety every government is obliged to guarantee its citizens. If the terrorists' playground is on social media, if extremism is now thriving online, if dissent and calls to arms and jihad have made social media their thriving ground, what is the impact and relevance of publicly condemning extremism and jihad?

Richards (2007) has also elaborated on the emotional origin of terrorism and its impact on the development of liberal democracies. He presented a case study of terrorism as a highly emotional topic and argued for a new style of political leadership, one which pays deliberate attention to the emotional dynamic of the publics the messages are aimed at. The role of PR, in its most basic and simplest form, is to engage the publics, to start a dialogue and to find a mutual language that all parties to that conversation can easily relate to and understand. If terrorists and their disciples speak about and are interested in a 'higher purpose' and a 'place which welcomes all', and the governments' dialogue content focuses on 'eradicating the extremist factions', then the opportunity to persuade and sway away terrorists from their intended targets and actions is missed.

Bleiker and Hutchinson (2008) suggest that nonviolent alternatives are rarely taken into consideration while addressing security issues, although they offer a vital understanding of terrorism and its counterstrategy. While these threats have become increasingly multifaceted and transnational, there is an eminent lack of dynamism in understanding and reacting to these issues. Like Richards, Blieker and Hutchinson firmly maintain that terrorism is an emotional issue. Just like a customer is not satisfied with his or her purchase and s/he does not believe that s/he received a good value for the money paid, the emotional roots of terrorism are, in their most basic form, related to a degree of personal satisfaction, purpose, respect and social acceptance.

Currently, the inability of the national governments across the Western democracies to find appropriate and compelling forms of spectacular response to terror in a value-based mode is stark. There are participatory arguments against terrorism in value-based communications, but these do not offer effective value-based 'symbols' of counterterrorism. According to Richards (2007), 'the public is impressed by moral worth or some other substantive value content (or the appearance thereof), not by sheer force.'

Alec Ross (2017), the former senior advisor for innovation to Hillary Clinton, argues that diplomats must have a far greater recognition of the agency of social media in reaching a public who now expect to be far more involved in diplomacy:

> we have done a horrendous job, a horrendous job, of maximising the potential of social media and technology to dial back violent extremism. ISIS and other terrorist organisations have had a much higher level of acumen using social media for radicalisation and recruitment. That's our one big failure.

Perhaps, although not the most optimal example of public diplomacy that can be given, it is Donald Trump the one who will change the current style of diplomatic discourse and engagement. According to the latest Twiplomacy study (2018):

> the U.S. President has also changed the tone of discourse on Twitter, frequently insulting his opponents and lampooning foreign leaders, calling North Korean leader Kim Jong-un "little rocket man," describing the Syrian president as a "gas killing animal," and threatening air strikes and war via tweets.

Twiplomacy's research found that 187 countries' heads of state and governments have 951 Twitter accounts between them. These countries represent 93% percent of the United Nations' member states, with a total of 324 million followers subscribing to their Twitter feeds. According to the same study, all European and South American countries have a presence on the social network, and even the Chinese government is becoming more amenable to social media engagement while some Chinese diplomatic missions are already engaging on Twitter, with the 'Chinese State Council Information Office maintaining a presence on Twitter, Facebook and YouTube'.

Social media has completely transformed the way in which we communicate and engage with one another. Risks are inherent and, nonetheless, considered acceptable for the access to free speech that social media provides. In this regard, W3C Technical Architecture Group argues that

> it is impossible to build systems that can securely support 'exceptional access' capabilities without breaking the trust guarantees of the web platform. Introducing such capabilities imposes known risks that far outweigh any hypothetical benefits. We initially set up the protocols in the internet and web stacks to optimise for sharing – we're only recently retrofitting security to it.
>
> (Beeman 2017)

Blaker (2015) argues that

> adolescents living in Western cultures have virtually no restrictions as to whom they connect and interact with when communicating over the Internet – and this is true for both Muslim and non-Muslim teens alike. Parents often have little, if any, knowledge of the contacts and associations their teens are making privately from their own computers and smartphones. For teenage girls raised in strict Muslim households who may, perhaps, live decidedly sheltered lives, behaviour that would be prohibited in their daily lives – communicating one-on-one with a young man without another male family member accompanying, for example – is completely feasible when the interaction occurs over the Internet.

Husna Haq (2014), a correspondent for The Christian Science Monitor, identified four reasons why American teens, in particular, are lured into joining the terrorists of the Islamic State, out of which the first two (mentioned below) are most indicative of the role played by social media in ISIS' recruitment:

- First, these groups can provide youth with a sense of identity. 'ISIS typically preys on Western youth who are disillusioned and have no sense of purpose or belonging.' This is similar to how urban gangs draw in disaffected, aimless youth, offering them a sense of family and purpose. 'The general picture provided by foreign fighters . . . suggests camaraderie, good morale and purposeful activity, all mixed in with a sense of understated heroism, designed to attract their friends as well as to boost their own self-esteem' (Barrett 2014).
- Second, ISIS operates a sophisticated propaganda machine (Haq 2014). Robert Hannigan, former director of GCHQ, stated that 'ISIS and other extremist groups use platforms like Twitter, Facebook and WhatsApp to reach their target audience in a language it understands. Their methods include exploiting popular hashtags to disseminate their message' (Mullen 2015). ISIS' use of social media allows for a quick distribution of propaganda messages and invites a widespread following.

Yasir Qadhi, a Muslim cleric in the US and professor at Rhodes College in Memphis, Tennessee, agrees that radicalisation occurs not in mosques but rather online, in secret. He relates that 'most parents are comfortable with a quieter Islam that tends to shy away from controversial matters, such as American policy in Muslim lands' (Reitman 2015). Consequently, there is a communication gap between generations. Aside from this communication gap, the technology and social media sites that adolescents use daily can be confusing and unfamiliar to their parents, guardians or other elder family members. There is an absence, Qadhi says, 'of genuine dialogue that could be tempered with some elderly wisdom' (Reitman 2015).

According to Jan Melissen (2016) of Clingendael, the Netherlands Institute on International Relations:

> social media make things more personal. And bring people who traditionally operate in the shadows into the limelight, giving an ambassador a face. You can find out what they are doing by following them on their social media account. People also get a more 'digital personality'.

According to Parmelee and Bichard (2012) 'tweets, too, may be framed with words or phrases that trigger positive or negative emotions in followers based on symbolism or other factors,' while one could argue that hashtags (#), especially on Twitter, have emerged as an effective way to share information and spur action about a demographic that seems to get little support from traditional mainstream media.

To explain the importance of emotional intelligence in combating terrorism, Awbrey (2006) argued the role world leadership should play in the counterterrorism effort. According to her, the real battlefield is in our minds, where terrorists are trying to create fear in big value – in this psychological warfare, the world leaders' first objective should be to help those most likely to be impacted regain control of their minds, with emotional intelligence being the main weapon of this battle.

Little attention is currently paid to the emotional part of terrorism. According to the International Society of Research Emotions (Kappas 2017), there is a lack of robustly applying emotion science to the study of terrorism-related emotions, from those of the recruits, to those of the victims, to those of the impacted society at large. Complex interdisciplinary research is required to understand what leads an educated English undergraduate to become a fierce killer like Jihadi John or to figure out what leads young French schoolgirls to get captivated by terrorists in a chat room to the point of joining ISIS.

Responding to violence with violence is not always the answer. While sharing his first-hand experience as an ISIS hostage, Henin (Guardian 2015) puts weight behind an emotion filled, non-violent spectacular response: 'they fear our unity, more than our air strikes.' He elaborates that in the aftermath of the Paris attacks, ISIS must have been pleased to see that the world has given them what they wanted in the shape of overreaction, division, fear, racism and xenophobia. Secondly, to spur their much-needed recruitment drive, they sought a higher loss of innocent lives in areas under their control as a result of more and more bombings.

Cohen (2016) identifies ISIS as the first terrorist organisation to use the internet with efficiency to spread its ideology and recruit followers in the region and abroad. The influx of ISIS-generated messages on Twitter can be gauged by the fact that in November 2014 there were around 46,000 ISIS-affiliated Twitter accounts broadcasting an average of 200,000 tweets per day (Berger and Morgan 2015) – as of August 2016, the numbers of ISIS-related accounts has significantly increased, reaching in excess of 200,000, with Twitter managing to successfully suspend 125,000 accounts with alleged links to ISIS.

ISIS has made the most of social media by forming a synergy of spectacle. Comparing ISIS' social media efforts with those of national and international counterterrorism efforts in value-based PR, two problems seem to surface: the first is the one related to credibility due to official involvement and the lack of spectacle. According to Roberts (2012), 'visual information increases credibility of a message. Pictures seem to hold more truth than words.' The other problem is the imminent dearth of intensity which is a hallmark of social media conversations. According to Fernandez (2015), 'it takes a network to fight a network' – the counterterrorism effort lacks the number of staff necessary to be able to compete with ISIS since ISIS' members and sympathisers numbers give a much bigger echo to its messages.

The challenge posed by ISIS to the 21st-century international community is different than the one the Taliban and Al-Qaeda posed in the 2001 Afghan

War. According to Louw (2003), the Western publics saw only the images the Pentagon wanted them to see, mainly because the Taliban were highly unskilled at responding to the Pentagon's PR game. During the Afghan War, the public saw images of sophisticated US weapons and carpet bombings ensuring the command and control of the US forces, with no images of the Taliban or civil casualties being broadcasted.

However, unlike the Taliban and Al-Qaeda, ISIS is far from lacking PR capabilities: its intensive presence on social media – especially Twitter – denied the US and wider members of the international community the PR/image control and embargo. Social media is ISIS' most powerful recruitment platform, and Ryan (2014) maintains that thousands of Westerners fighting alongside ISIS in Syria and Iraq are a reflection of ISIS' smart use of Twitter and Facebook. The live nature of these two social media platforms enabled ISIS to reach disillusioned Westerners and provide them with a sense of community.

ISIS' recruitment success is continuously showcased via Twitter since the foreign recruits are the biggest motivation for the newcomers. According to Weimann and McCants (2014), the social media profiles of Western recruits are presented inclusive of their nationality, which is usually mentioned after their new Muslim names given to them by ISIS. This level of authenticity displayed by ISIS members in their recruitment practices across the social platforms is very similar to the current (yet not fully exploited) trends of employee engagement and employee advocacy for brand recognition and awareness.

Just as ISIS was and still is a 'brand', its members are its 'employees'. Any respectable organisation puts its employees first and uses these employees to further the credibility and recognition of its corporate values, mission and ethos – as if taken from a textbook on best practice PR, ISIS did just that.

Girl Talk (2014) asserts that

> the increased social media recruitment efforts of women in the Islamic State to get higher numbers of women to move to Syria indicate an agenda beyond militaristic goals. As such, female-run social media accounts describe a purposeful life in Syria while also providing information explaining how to enter the state – women view themselves not only as educators of the Islamic State's youth, but also as crucial agents in adding to its population.

However, according to the International Centre for the Study of Radicalisation and Political Violence (ICSR), in February 2015, ISIS published 892 propaganda pieces – videos, photos, audio content and written articles – across their digital output. In the same month of 2017, their number of propaganda materials fell to 570, a decline of 36% (Cheshire 2017). It could be argued that a heightened policing of the social media platforms by their owners as well as the various security and intelligence apparatus led to this decrease.

Charlie Winter (Cheshire 2017), a senior research fellow at ICSR, told Sky News:

> It's much more difficult now to stumble across Islamic State propaganda, there's no question of that. But the brand is still out there. So, through terrorism, through adopting attacks like that carried outside the Houses of Parliament on Wednesday, ISIS is actually able to use that as propaganda, it's able to use those attacks as a way to keep itself at the forefront of people's minds. And, in that sense, propaganda and terrorism are one and the same thing for Islamic State.

ISIS, as briefly highlighted in this literature review chapter, has proved to the international community that its online threat, due to its continuous and difficult-to-disrupt nature, poses many more dangers than the actual war on the ground in Syria and Iraq. ISIS' approach to and engagement in mass communication across genders, ages, nationalities and geographies is unconventional and totally unprecedented for extremist groups – it has caught the international community by surprise and unprepared, grappling to understand how to position itself in the light of these new rules of engagement, made even more complex by the difficulty of having a direct dialogue with the online communities that represent, one could argue, the extremists' 'hunting ground'.

2

21ST-CENTURY CHALLENGES

Internet and social media

Beginning in 1993, when former American vice president Al Gore announced the appearance of *information highways*, a large body of literature has been struggling to identify the promises and dangers of this information network that was started in the United States and, soon after, engulfed the planet. Initially meant to be used for scientific exchanges between university professors, the World Wide Web became highly coveted by a variety of actors – governments and terrorists, too – from a political, economic and ideological point of view due to its unrestricted access (Leiner et al. 2016).

Defense Advanced Research Projects Agency's (DARPA) scientists put together a timeline of the internet evolution and are also currently running a project on social media in strategic communication which 'seeks to develop tools to help identify misinformation or deception campaigns and counter them with truthful information, reducing one's ability to manipulate events' (Sanchez 2016).

Social media platforms, which have risen due to the growth of the internet, first began to appear around 2004–2005. Well-known instances where these platforms have played a significant role in facilitating or repressing social unrest have occurred even more recently. The political novelty of these cases has been matched only by the accelerating frequency with which they are suddenly cropping up in a wide variety of authoritarian countries around the world.

The suddenness of social media's relevance and impact has surprised both Western governments and authoritarian regimes and, sometimes, even the civil societies and dissidents themselves (Aistrope 2016:121), with the two main social media platforms in use worldwide being Facebook and Twitter.

One could argue that, for democratic governments, social media platforms largely play a dissemination role: one where the government-generated information can be furthered amplified to ensure that all segments of society are reached, and information is timely received. For authoritarian governments, social media represents mainly a monitoring station from where they could quickly 'extract' the dissenting voices of the so-called troublemakers. Sina Weibo, for instance, China's own version of Twitter, has been created and allowed to exist simply because it can be fully monitored by the Chinese authorities since Twitter itself and Facebook are blocked completely in mainland China (Koetse 2015).

Facebook is the largest and most ubiquitous social networking website on the internet today. Developed in 2003, Facebook has since expanded significantly; the company opened its international headquarters in 2008 with an active user base of 100 million and now boasts 2.27 billion monthly active users (Abbruzzese 2018). More than 75% of Facebook users are located outside the US and are able to create personal, group and event pages and then post photos, videos and text entries to other pages, as well as chat in real-time, exchange private messages and share longer messages with other users (Rozumski 2015), unlike Twitter's previous limit of 140 characters (as of November 2017, 280 characters are now allowed).

Twitter is the second-most-used social media platform in the world. Established in 2006, it is a popular social networking and micro-blogging service through which users can send and receive text-based posts of up to 280 characters, known informally as 'tweets'. Although it was launched over a decade ago, Twitter has expanded most rapidly in the last three years – as of December 2018, Twitter generated over 500 million tweets a day (Cooper 2019).

Political observers and actors, who used to base their strategies and policies on more traditional and predictable diplomatic factors, have struggled to adjust to the sudden emergence of these new online, virtual platforms of interaction. At times, even academic and government experts have been surprised by the urgency of social media, a problem often compounded by generational gaps and a general lack of technological familiarity with digital tools. This was perhaps epitomized just a few days after the 2009 Green Movement protests first began breaking out in Iran. Although global media coverage of internet-powered protest movements quickly exploded following the 2009 Iranian protests, this coverage has also itself come under harsh criticism (Kamal and Chu 2012).

Some authoritarian governments have quickly adapted to these technological developments by adopting a variety of customised and sophisticated responses, ranging from China's Orwellian policy of massive censorship and surveillance infrastructure to drastic decisions taken in places such as Libya and Egypt to turn off the internet entirely during moments of civil unrest (Law 2016).

The political impact of the internet and new social media tools on the modern-day struggle between authoritarian regimes and civil societies has been enhanced by the internet's expansion and by the manner in which it is creating different ways of communicating and disseminating information (Hai-Jew 2017).

The rapid proliferation and near-universal utility of social media have helped catalyse recent outbreaks of social unrest across a wide spectrum of countries and regions around the world. The details, domestic factors, and outcomes of these conflicts have varied greatly. Social media's impact in these struggles has, likewise, differed significantly (Richards 2016).

Noteworthy in this regard is the social activism and strong influence exercised by Srdja Popovic, one of the founders of the non-violent resistance group 'Otpor' whose social campaigns led to Slobodan Milosevic's demise in 2000. Today, building on his deep knowledge of social epidemics, non-violent activism and mass mobilisation, Popovic is the co-founder and chairman of the Centre for Applied Nonviolent Action and Strategies at Harvard's Kennedy School. His work has also been cited as highly influential by the activists involved in the Arab Spring movement in 2011.

Some examples of social media's diversity include its central role in mobilising the revolution that ultimately toppled the Mubarak regime in Egypt, its disputed role in Iran's failed Green Revolution, its positive but minimal footprint in anti-authoritarian protests in Yemen and its employment as an important avenue both for challenging as well as for entrenching ruling political parties in Russia and China. This diversity offers observers, researchers and analysts a rich vein for extrapolating common trends and characteristics about how and when social media proliferation challenges or empowers authoritarian governments (Miladi 2016:285).

The internet has grown and evolved to create a set of technologies that allowed a shift from the traditional categories of web content publishing, such as the Britannica or personal websites, to an era of collaborative projects such as blogs, internet public pages and articles (Law 2016).

In July 2010, seven years after its launch, Facebook announced that it had reached half a billion users, leading *The Economist* to wonder whether the popular platform was eroding or even encroaching upon the traditional conception of a sovereign nation-state, with social media networks reportedly adding about 400,000 new users a day, helping transform the way news is gathered and distributed, reshaping how public figures communicate and playing a significant role in popular protests in Iran, China, Egypt, Tunis and Moldova (Rozumski 2015).

The internet has not only facilitated increased communication and interaction among a nation's citizens, but it has also encouraged a growing degree of linkage between the civil societies and social movements of different countries. The internet is seen to be a perfect fit for the increasingly transnational nature of political and cultural issues, leading some scholars to point to the transition to a more complex, global, information-based society that almost logically shapes the context for new forms of online activism (Rozumski 2015).

International community

International communication differs from interpersonal communication – how heads of state and government behave and act in a public setting is different from the way they would act in private. In an interconnected globalised society, barriers seem to be built more often than they are taken down. As Sartre (2003) argued, private individuals put on a show, to some extent and in certain situations, for others to believe, understand and agree to their demands.

There is little difference between the formal diplomatic communication and that of corporate communication. Just like diplomats, chief executive officers (CEOs) of many corporations cannot afford to express their personal views and opinions on a variety of matters without careful consideration. What they say and do can have significant repercussions on the diplomatic relationships between their countries and those of their counterparts (in the diplomats' case) or on the share value or market share of their corporations (in the CEOs' case).

Governments have found that simply being present is not enough to influence the masses. Participation in the online debate is the critical factor that can turn the diplomatic efforts of the governments into powerful diplomacy results. The internet provides a new platform for the traditional practice of diplomacy in the international realm, and three aspects become crucial in exploiting the new medium: a presence, participation in debate and the extent of connection. The international community groups that are visible across all communication platforms and engage in public debate will yield more influence on the international diplomacy stage.

A very recent example in this regard was an experiment recently (Fleming 2019) run by the North Atlantic Treaty Organization (NATO) that used fake Facebook accounts to trick soldiers into sharing sensitive information. While the results of the experiment are unnerving in terms of soldiers having been successfully tricked to disclose that information, what is noteworthy is the fact that the experiment seems to have proved that it was possible to directly influence people's actions and behaviour by making those soldiers abandon their posts while on duty.

International relations, viewed through the lens of PR and social media engagement, are paramount in steering the direction of the local, national, regional and international discourse. However, irrespective of how well planned, structured or organised such communication activities may be, today's international relations at the level of nation-states and sovereign powers seem to be lacking what social media platforms and users mostly appreciate: the emotional, human component (Castells 2013).

Public relations (PR) is both an art and a science. The art requires a complex mix of specific skills that should be targeted to and deployed in specific situations, accompanied by a mix of relevant tools (style, nuance, rhetoric, language, argument) and platforms (print media, social media channels, TV, radio, podcasts etc.). The science of PR relates to techniques involved in the research, analysis and positioning of the means used by its art. PR does not have a 'one size fits all' approach as government communication does – everything is tailored and situation specific, and the results are measured and aligned to the objectives of the communication requirement.

In a diplomatic setting, public behaviour and communication are the products of a very careful deliberation and organisation. When in public, the official is always under scrutiny, and his/her actions must be gauged appropriately. One cannot confound the personal means of communication and engagement with those displayed at state level: the latter are not spontaneous and are eminently political in nature (Schmidt and Cohen 2013).

The state must be sensitive to the impression its representatives (civil servants, embassy staff, government employees) make on observers. In international affairs, what these state representatives say and do is interpreted as being the formal position of their respective governments. No personal input, attachment, comments or gestures can be made – there is no room for personal error; even in the case of diplomatic faux pas, such errors are seldom – if ever – attributed to a lack of knowledge or to a moment of human weakness (Schmidt and Cohen 2013). This is why social media engagement and digital diplomacy are becoming of paramount importance in international affairs – today, hearts and minds can be won where they hold their main conversations: on social media, not in Whitehall, Capitol Hill or Brussels.

Public officials cannot express their personal views, only those of the government offices they represent and work for. This public-communication conundrum has never been more poignant than today – democratic governments want to engage with their citizens, while the citizens are becoming less and less interested in engaging with the governments and, even more so, their official representatives (Rutter 2014). The paradox of political and governmental engagement seems to have been further widened by the current US president (Donald Trump) whose persona, for many of his voters and supporters in the US and across the world, seems to trump that of the office he represents. Citizens do want to engage with the political and ruling classes – but they want to speak with and communicate with the individual office-holders, not with the office the latter have sworn allegiance to.

The modern means of communication are no longer restricted to national territory. Nations seem to struggle to be represented in the conversations taking place across so many platforms, and the state's monopoly on culture and information has weakened (Hurn and Tomalin 2013:16). The democratic ideal values the fact that ordinary individuals can express themselves, and such an expression may replace a search for the truth. It can therefore be argued that where an 'explosion' in communication occurs, such an explosion does not suppress the reasoning or the gist of the debate – it only complicates it.

While conventional diplomacy has been primarily concerned with the geographical borders, today's conflicts – given the rise of fundamentalist extremism – force us to take into consideration the individuals' 'inner-borders': what someone believes in, stands for, aspires to and wishes to. The 21st century has made the globalised society face a stark reality, namely that the acceptance and absorption of cultural and religious diversity in and between societies are imperative. The diplomatic actors are changing fast, and presidents, prime ministers and various government and diplomatic officials are now subject to the general public's acceptance and endorsement, their 'public mandate' being constantly under scrutiny.

Pandith argued that 'the credible voices we need to bring up have to come from non-Government faces, and the kinds of people who need to work on the campaigns can't be the government' (Philps 2015). And Pandith couldn't be more correct – people relate to and believe in people like themselves and those they look up to. A family member or a friend, even a pillar of the physical or the online community, can exert significantly more influence on specific masses than any president, prime minister or government official ever could.

The speed and ubiquity of media channels, primarily those related to social media platforms, have accelerated diplomatic actions, thus giving rise to what is currently known as 'megaphone diplomacy' (Sparre 2001:88). Conventional diplomacy's approach to social media is becoming increasingly favourable, paying more attention to the social chatter and using it to inform its potential state-level actions.

In a globalised age, the opportunity and need to stay in touch and be 'connected' 24/7 are constantly increasing. These emerging tendencies apply not only to private individuals whose number, according to the data available (Hootsuite 2019), has reached almost 4.4 billion internet users, but to governments, too. As per the findings of a study (2015) done by the Organisation for Economic Co-operation and Development (OECD) into the scope and usage of social media by central governments, a growing segment of the population is expecting their government to be present on social media platforms and to share relevant information on such platforms. According to the same findings, the development of governments' social media accounts has seen a dramatic increase during the study's reference period of 2014–2015, with Afghanistan, Saudi Arabia and India topping the chart.

From a PR, communication and public engagement perspective, this dramatic governmental shift towards unconventional forms of diplomatic communication could be ascribed to the citizens' need to stay informed and be informed. To this end, and as argued by Legget (2017):

> social media was vital to the delivery of Paris Climate Summit and I've seen it gain more and more importance since the Copenhagen Climate Summit in 2009, and I think it was vital in delivering a 'Treaty with teeth' and that has never happened before in history.

Today, the public expects the governments to keep them informed of their international activities. The traditional forms of media consumption (newspapers, TV, radio and magazines) are no longer the masses' preferred sources of information – social media platforms are, while the trust in traditional media is continuing to erode (Oster 2018).

Social media has permanently changed the way in which groups act, react and mobilise. Le Bon (2014) argued that crowds are not impressed by reason but only by a 'startling and very clear image, freed from all accessory explanation'. The postulates of mass communication also argue that symbols cannot move groups – they cannot evoke shared assumptions, sentiments or basic emotions and abide by the principles of a collective purpose or sense of belonging; it is the human feelings that need to be tapped into (Cohen 1985).

Lord William Wallace of Saltaire (2016) argued that

> symbolism matters in foreign policy as much as the personal relations matter for Heads of State and Prime Ministers. Empathy in international relations is very important and cross-cultural awareness is often overlooked. Recently, it has been the social media that did make a difference in foreign policy – the internet has hugely contributed to general members of the public finding information as quickly as the Governments themselves do. The internet has dramatically altered the balance of the international relations dialogue.

Bridget Kendall (2016), the former BBC diplomatic correspondent, said that 'the rise of social media is already changing the principles of conventional diplomacy, of dialogue between nation states and international organisations.' Moreover, according to Baroness Ashton (2016), 'today we see challenges as individual nations as well as group nations – in 2009, the Arab Spring and the overthrow of the Ghaddafi regime in Libya seemed unconceivable.' One clear consequence of social media is that people in one country can learn about and gain inspiration from what is going on elsewhere. Further investigation into how groups or governments can seek to influence what is going on in another country and how they do this by using a variety of means at their disposal – including an unethical and inappropriate PR approach, similar to Bell Pottinger's activities in South Africa in 2017 – may be a research area for further books or academic papers on this matter.

Michael Kaiser, the executive director of the US National Cyber Security Alliance argues that 'one of the greatest strengths of social networks is that they are platforms for free speech.' However, he notes, 'people who are up to no good will use any communication vehicle available' to get their message out (Nichols, Stein and Daniels 2015). Additionally, in his 'Plan for a Free and Open Internet', the former US president Barack Obama said that 'an open Internet is crucial to America's very way of life.' He added that 'by lowering the cost of launching a new idea, igniting new political movements and bringing communities closer together, the Internet has been one of the most significant democratizing influences the world has ever known' (White House 2016).

As of February 2017, Twitter was used by heads of state and governments of 173 countries (BBC Radio 2017) – and digital diplomacy is, it seems, an indispensable communication tool for governments. Alec Ross argues (BBC 2017) that

> we're moving into a world where statecraft is not just something done by white men wearing white shirts and red ties, behind closed doors, with a cup of coffee in hand – technology and networks are increasingly disrupting the power structures and the relationships between states.

Mr Trump's (US president) vehement attacks on Twitter against his North Korean counterpart are a matter of public notoriety, surprising no one anymore – his uncanny use of social media, especially Twitter, as well as his raw authenticity (or show?), will highly likely be a topic of study for many years to come. Analysing Mr Trump's tweets in 2018, Politico (2018) created a superb interactive map unveiling the ratio between the US president's attacks and promotional content on Twitter, with the attacks unsurprisingly yielding a much higher number than any matter of public interest he chose to present. His popularity is not waning, nor has his diatribe been taken seriously (so far) by any of America's known enemies and allies. One of the reasons may well be that social media, for the time being, is not considered by the diplomatic corps a proper formal form of bilateral dialogue or international discourse – perhaps the time is long overdue to reconsider this position.

Social media behaviours and interactions, other than being a constant source of information gathering for fundamentalist extremists or organised crime networks, also represent an invaluable source of data-gathering for security and intelligence experts across the world. Social media facilitates the constructions and predictions of behavioural patterns of groups and online circles, thus greatly contributing to crafting strategic short-, mid- and long-term actions and narratives for governments, diplomats and members of the intelligence community.

However, there is a valid counterargument to be made: had there been social media platforms in 1979, is it likely that the foreign intelligence failure during Iran's Islamic Revolution could have been totally averted since the foreign diplomats only found out about the population's dissent and the various pockets of street protests when it was too late? Perhaps the answer to this question is yes – a sentiment analysis of the masses could have been performed by using a variety of social media analytics tools, one which could have been easily validated by formal means of sociological research, i.e. interviews, ad-hoc surveys, focus groups and targeted information-gathering as well as a variety of other techniques deployed by the intelligence services.

As the internet continues to expand and as usage and access increase, the online environment will almost certainly become 'a virtual battleground' (Schmidt and Cohen 2013). Information has always been part of the war fighter's arsenal, and the capabilities of the internet, unlike any other communication platforms, far outstretch its capacity as the world's greatest information resource or as the most diverse facilitator of communication.

It could be argued that the internet and social media did not overhaul the principles of democracy and international co-operation – they have simply made them more pertinent than ever. Democracies continue to face the same challenge they always have, balancing their citizens' security and protection with freedoms and values. However, what social media did bring, and what the international community is not entirely prepared for, is a complete change of scenery of the fundamental battle for hearts and minds: this is no longer taking place in war trenches or conventional battlefields. Today, the battle for emotions and human reactions is primarily taking place in a virtual place, one which no government in the world has been fully successful in embargoing, controlling or leading: on social media.

Walker (2015:20) argued that 'the online space allows Muslim communities to bypass those institutions, both religious and cultural, that they feel do not represent them.' The lack of physical boundaries and the near impossibility of curbing content online have led to the flourishing of typically censored material, although the 21st-century globalised world needs information – between nation-states, businesses, international organisations and social actors.

Digital communications have made our century's information-exchange landscape fast and unpredictable. With such an ease of information flow, there is a need – condemned by many – to control not the quantity of information but the quality thereof. As much as social media and the internet can contribute to development and progress, they can also cause instability and uncertainty: two of the most undesirable aspects of diplomacy and international relations.

In March 2015, the former US president Obama said: 'We can't keep on thinking about counterterrorism and security as entirely separate from diplomacy, development, education – all these things that are considered soft but, in fact, are vital to our national security' (Zenko 2015). Poverty and lack of education, in and of themselves, do not cause terrorism (Stern 2015). However, it has been empirically proven that terrorist groups often exploit the uncertainty surrounding developing or underdeveloped countries, failed governments and, primarily, past totalitarian or dictatorship states.

The rise of ISIS changed the narrative and approach of Western governments towards Islamic fundamentalism. The change brought by the rise of ISIS has completely changed the rules of the game – the psychological mastery deployed by the group, corroborated with an impeccable skill in using the traditional and modern platforms of mass communication, meant that ISIS' propaganda machine still is and was unrivalled. ISIS has a brand: that brand is striving to disseminate and present its 'caliphate', and its media production teams cater to a vast and culturally diverse audience ranging from Central Asia to West Africa and from Europe to America.

One of the latest reviews on countering violent extremism published by the Institute for Strategic Dialogue (Briggs and Feve 2013)

> demonstrated that solutions to violent extremist messaging cannot be the work of government alone, they must be a partnership between states, civil society, and the international community. It is only when state and non-state organizations make a deliberate effort to explain their actions in light of a strategic narrative that they can make effective strides in countering extremist messaging. Doing anything else leaves a powerful stage open to actors who do not deserve the spotlight.

In the autumn of 2015, a new Commonwealth Counter Extremism Unit was launched to 'focus on strengthening the ability of Commonwealth countries to counter extremist narrative' through 'new approaches to countering poisonous ideologies', with one of its top priorities being the development of 'capacity-building through non-governmental organisations' (UK Government 2015).

Given that the 'poisonous ideologies' referred to above are primarily shared across social media channels, as evidenced elsewhere in this book, it can therefore be argued that a concerted and sustained social media engagement is necessary to counteract extremist narratives such as ISIS'.

Social media matters, or should matter, for today's international relations and diplomacy, especially since more and more diplomats, academics and intelligence analysts are making the case for the necessity of mass engagement. As argued throughout this book, social media platforms have surpassed the other means of public communication such as newspapers, periodicals, TV and radio – the people, the influencers, the extremists and the non-governmental actors can all be found in one location: on social media. According to Mark Wallace (2015), the CEO of the Counter Extremism Project and former US ambassador to the United Nations, 'Twitter is the gate to cyber jihad, where many eventual recruits have the first taste of extremist propaganda and recruitment.'

It is this global ultra-connectedness brought about by social media that can backfire in nefarious ways since 'it can make it easier to build a silo than ever before,' as argued by University of Michigan psychologist Dr Richard Nisbett (Maney 2014). 'On social networks, it is easy to block out people who don't think like you', Nisbett explains, 'and strengthen the connection with people who share your outlook. You can reach across the globe to find like-minded people and build your own echo-chamber.' This 'echo-chamber' was put to best use by ISIS and its extremists to attract more and more supporters and incite disenfranchised youth to acts of terrorism across Europe, Middle East and United States.

Knowledge of the mechanics of social epidemics may enable ethnical identities to be engineered – people's behaviours can be manipulated and their voting intentions changed entirely to serve the purposes of others, as clearly evidenced by the outcome of the UK's European Union membership referendum of 2016. Using similar psychological and emotional levers and triggers such as those used by the 'Leave Campaign', especially those related to one of the most fundamental human feelings – fear – the images proliferated by ISIS across the social media platforms have sowed terror among many and admiration among few. The picture of a beheaded Westerner has a much stronger psychological impact on the hearts and minds of the masses than the image of a G8 members' summit, just like the prospect of a jobless father of three in the UK's Great Yarmouth (BBC 2016) has because of a large amount of Eastern European 'cheap labour'.

It was social media that allowed ISIS to thrive and expand; it was social media that proliferated ISIS' call to arms; and it was social media that gave rise to a new type of jihad, one for which no textbook has been written yet: how the jihad, a highly totalitarian and extremist social movement, can expand its reach and number of fighters by using one of the most democratic forms of expression of the 21st century, namely the freedom of speech.

ISIS – a modern-day style of jihad

For ISIS, the most recent 'product' of Middle Eastern states' inability and/or unwillingness to address violent extremism, 'statehood' is not a utopian concept – it is the ultimate goal of its fight, mission and creed. The latest updated report of the Soufan Group on ISIS (2017) – 'Beyond the Caliphate: Foreign Fighters and the Threat of Returnees' – indicates that there are '40,000 foreigners who flocked to join IS from more than 110 countries both before and after the declaration of the caliphate in June 2014'. Of these, the same report ascertains that approximately '5,600 citizens or residents from 33 countries' have returned home.

The fact that these recruits are and were nationals of more than 110 countries is testament to the significant attraction ISIS' messages have regardless of their manner or channel of dissemination – they address and target a disenfranchised segment of the population, mostly youth. ISIS was, and still is, providing its recruits with a promise: that of a new state with new rules, one where the West's influence and judgement cannot reach, one where Western values have no place.

Farah Pandit (Philps 2015), adjunct senior fellow at the Council on Foreign Relations, argues that extremist groups are taking advantage of an 'identity crisis' among young people, particularly among young Muslim men and women living in a post-9/11 world. 'Extremists are using that crisis of identity to shape the way in which they try to seduce an online space,' she notes, further emphasizing that these groups work like an advertising agency – 'selling an ideology in a visual way' – and tailoring messages to create a mirror image between recruiter and recruit.

Social media – while mostly used by its 3.5 billion users across the world for peaceful purposes – was and is employed by ISIS to attract followers, create fear and panic among the masses and portray an image of intangibility (Wired 2016). While ISIS has a very clear on-the-ground presence in Iraq and Syria, with various cells spread across Europe, Africa and Central Asia, its real stronghold is the internet: the place where conventional diplomacy, international relations and diplomatic conventions have failed to gain ground.

While in the past terrorist groups were finding it difficult to engage with their members and supporters due to a strict monitoring by the intelligence services of conventional communication networks, today the interaction with their group members and sympathisers could not be easier. With the click of a button, a message cannot only be sent to one person – it can be sent to thousands and shared by millions.

ISIS' messages have reached much higher numbers of people than they would have in the pre-internet age. The emergence of Web 2.0, and of social media platforms in particular, led to many more individuals being able to be reached and targeted by ISIS' propaganda machine compared to its predecessors, who only had websites and online jihadi forums to rely on. The impact assessment and likelihood of impact are very simple: the greater the number of people exposed to

ISIS-generated media content, the higher the number of individuals likely to be influenced, in some way, by that content.

It is much easier to find jihadi content online today than it was even seven or eight years ago; one no longer needs a high level of internet literacy or Arabic language skills. In fact, on many social media platforms (given their cookie policies, geolocation capacity and various data analysis/online streaming algorithms), once one locates a profile or any piece of content that may be of interest, that person will be 'recommended' similar content to look at and so on; these 'recommendations' work in the same way for extremist- and ISIS-related content as they do for any other general consumption videos/advertisements.

In 2010, a then unknown Google marketing executive created a Facebook page highlighting violent citizen suppression by Egyptian authorities. That action catalysed a massive 250,000-strong political movement which, within months, led to regime change. It was during those days of 2010 that an Egyptian activist tweeted (BBC Radio 4 2017), 'we use Facebook to schedule a protest, Twitter to co-ordinate and YouTube to tell the world.' 21st-century social movements will not just be televised – they will be tweeted, streamed and Instagrammed. Social media remains an incredible force for good, but, as will be further evidenced in this book, it also is a powerful means of manipulation, propaganda, terror and recruitment.

In December 2015, a video was released by ISIS showing children armed with pistols and playing hide-and-seek, hunting bound captives before killing them. A novel form of assassination – even for ISIS – featured in their latest media productions before the liberation of Raqqa from ISIS' occupation: captives dressed in orange clothes were taken off to the sea, thrown from boats with their hands and feet tied, with rocks being thrown at them so they could die an even slower and more painful death. Such gruesome and gripping images were made much easier to 'rejoice' in and share by ISIS' supporters since an updated version of the ISIS app (yes, their 'media department' has even created an app to ensure message amplification and optimisation across handheld devices) was launched in early 2016, allowing its users an instant download of such 'promotional' materials (Alcorn 2016).

And to make images more appealing, regardless of their incredibly cruel nature, the musical department of ISIS also released a public catchy jihadist chant (*nasheed*) in Mandarin Chinese (Osborne 2015) entitled 'I am a Mujahid' – after all, ISIS has been run (and still is) as a multinational corporation with 'stakeholder groups' in a variety of countries speaking different languages. Their 'products' need and needed to be appropriately targeted and suitable for the national profile of their potential recruits – just as the PR and marketing department of any multinational corporation would do.

It is the rise of ISIS that led to the international community's intervention in Syria, since it has been rightly concluded by the world's superpowers that the Middle East could not withstand another wave of extremism after the devastation caused by Al-Qaeda in the region. ISIS, without a doubt, was – and still is to some extent – a real regional threat. Its greatest threat of all is not its ability to infiltrate the Western way of life and carry out surgical terrorist attacks on the civilian population but its recruitment practices – by using online forums and state-of-the-art communication systems and engagement skills, ISIS has had its notoriety and appeal soar.

Twitter has been shutting down thousands of suspect ISIS accounts since 2015, and YouTube has increased its vigilance in terms of the video content uploaded by its registered users, with any 'inappropriate' content being taken down much faster than before. Most importantly, Telegram – an online messaging service – has been blocking the ISIS' 'PR machine' since November 2015, although not totally successfully since some messages do still manage to get through. A very clear step forward in curbing apps, such as Telegram, from being used has been taken by Apple, which removed the app from its App Store (Field 2018).

With the support of the current Syrian president – Bashar al-Assad – ISIS successfully managed to set up its communication centre in Raqqa (Griffing 2018), and the technology it used (and is still using) is making it harder and harder to track it since ISIS had been constantly banished from mainstream social media platforms (although not completely successfully). ISIS' removal from 'mainstream' consumption has brought along an unwanted effect: that of ISIS having to shift its propaganda onto the dark web, a hard-to-trace part of the internet largely inaccessible to ordinary web browsers, a place where it is exceptionally difficult for the authorities to intervene and remove content.

The symbolism of ISIS executing foreigners was and still is very powerful, aimed at frightening the world's democracies. ISIS' leaders have been engaged in mass cultural productions, every single communication output being modelled on the trajectory of the Prophet Muhammad's life, i.e. 'God has spoken'. According to its leader – and proved correct by the events of the last six years – Abu Bakr al Baghdadi, ISIS does not need a territorial state to be a state because ISIS is 'a state of believers', and, although ISIS may have been thrown out from its occupied cities in Iraq and Syria, 'the land of Allah is wide and the tides of war change' (Callimachi 2018).

Terrorists started crowdsourcing funds or using digital media for propaganda before most counterterrorist international units had even begun to understand the capabilities the technological transformation of the late 1990s had brought (Withnall 2014). There is evidence that ISIS floated the idea of declaring a caliphate on social media to test the potential reaction among other extremists, and they may have even approached senior Al-Qaeda commanders (Barrett 2014) to check their appetite for joining forces with ISIS. What is very interesting in terms of this 'testing' approach is that ISIS, just like any PR or marketing campaign for a product/service launch, used social media platforms to validate its proposition and its appeal to its target 'customers'.

As new media technologies and changes in the way in which images can be produced and circulated, shared and disseminated have seen a formidable increase, it becomes increasingly difficult to understand war, violence and terrorism without taking visual media into account (Friis 2015:725), a trend that had begun before the rise of social media. The circulation of visual stories of (alleged) attacks to incite either public support for a country's intervention or international support for action had been successfully used in the Iraq War and the civil wars in former Yugoslavia. NGOs, especially those with a charitable remit, have equally used visual aids in their efforts to incentivise and sensitise the members of the public to donate.

As exemplified by the widespread circulation of ISIS' extremely gruesome videos, corroborated with actual visual accounts of the destruction of UNESCO World Heritage Sites in Iraq and mass graves in Syria, the technological innovations of the digital age have not only influenced just how romanticised horror can be presented to the online communities but, if presented properly, how attractive this can be for a certain segment of the disenfranchised Muslim population.

Through social and mainstream media (Stern and Berger 2016:36), ISIS has taken public terror to new levels by widely displaying the blood-drenched results of their operations across social media channels, platforms guaranteed to reach hundreds of millions of users across the world. The terrorist group has caught the international community's attention with its rapid expansion in Syria and Iraq by publicising the brutal treatment of non-Sunni believers and, in particular, the non-Muslim faiths and those who are found to go against ISIS' beliefs (Steed 2016).

It is important to point out that ISIS' members are not the first violent extremists or terrorists to harness the power of the internet – far from it. In fact, Neo-Nazis, the Ku Klux Klan and other extreme right-wing groups were some of the first to do politics 'online,' using bulletin board systems (BBS), in the early to mid-1980s. Most major terrorist groups established an online presence between the mid-1990s and 2000s.

Through social media, ISIS has been given the opportunity to show beheadings of hostages, to livestream public executions, to present an idyllic image of the life inside the 'caliphate' and to romanticise the role of children in a battle to win disciples. ISIS has proved to be very savvy in its use of social media, with teams working to create crafted statements with accompanying videos or images that showcase ISIS' accomplishments and spread its propaganda (Atwan 2015).

According to Jenkins (2016), 'each terrorist group has its repertoire, its modus operandi. The IRA does not engage in plane hijackings or abductions. Italy's Red Brigades used to shoot media representatives in their legs, while German terrorists are known to be meticulous planners.' ISIS, unlike the more traditional terrorist factions, does not have a preferred method of execution – it does, however, have preferred methods of communicating its executions, and social media channels are ISIS' stage to the world.

In his *Art of War*, Sun-Tzu (2014) argued that by killing one, a thousand can be terrorised. It can thus be inferred that the victim(s) are less important than the general effect terrorist acts produce – the impact across a variety of unwilling and unparticipating spectators is stark: the means of mass communication, the fastest ones being the internet and the social media platforms, ensure the propagation of such acts is almost immediate. In a society hungry for sensational news of any kind, grotesque and gut-wrenching human suffering elicits the most attention.

Due to the increased number of social media accounts and the highly successful use of the 'dark net' that ISIS fighters use, the United Nations argued that it is hard to pin down all the social media accounts that are used by ISIS or to detect any accounts that are used to spread ISIS propaganda (Martin 2000), especially since social media has led to the rebranding of ISIS' mission of terrorism into an appealing subculture, especially for the young Muslims who believe that, by making the ultimate sacrifice and giving their lives for the ISIS' cause, they will enjoy a better afterlife.

In a study carried out by Trussler and Soroka (2014) on 'Consumer Demand for Cynical and Negative News Frames', it was evidenced that, 'regardless of their preferences, . . . participants are more likely to select negative content', making the humans' negativity bias and attraction towards inappropriate social behaviour a current subject of psychological academic research. ISIS, instead of shocking and upsetting the Muslim congregations across the world, has achieved the opposite: it has attracted many, too many, Muslims to its call for action.

The United Nations also cites online spaces as potential sources of radicalisation and a primary concern for international security. Social media platforms such as Facebook and Twitter function as radicalising forums within which young people are introduced to pro-jihadist messages, networked to others with similar reinforcing views and, in some cases, actively recruited to join Islamic terrorist groups (Elson 2012). Therefore, social media is the medium through which the ideology of obedience to Allah has led to an increase in the number of people who want to join ISIS (Al-Barghouti 2008).

Although much has been written on various aspects of this phenomenon, there is one propagandistic device frequently found on social media sites that has generated little attention: the subversion of popular messages to propagate pro-terrorist messages, a mechanism known as political disruption (Barrett 2014). As such, some social media messages from ISIS focussed on successful attacks or on killing individuals who have been captured or found guilty of some imaginary offence (Faris and Rahimi 2015) against the rules of the caliphate.

The advancement of internet technologies has brought different dimensions to the way in which ISIS operates (Williams 2016). Through social media platforms, ISIS could easily – and still can to a certain extent – spread propaganda and fear among the international community. Since social media's sole purpose is that of being used as a platform of multi-party communication and engagement (Cockburn 2016), ISIS' members could use these platforms to, on the one hand, spread threats targeted to the international community and, on the other hand, attract and enchant new recruits from across the world.

Of most concern to the international community should be the ease with which ISIS can easily spread propaganda across social media platforms and how this terror militia masterfully manipulates the media, encouraging people from a variety of backgrounds, nationalities and socio-economic profiles to fight in the name of and join the Islamic State (Cockburn 2016).

Today, there seems to be a direct relationship and proportionality between the intensity of the fight against ISIS and the seemingly endless war of tackling ISIS on social media platforms (Turley 2014). Data gathered from a significant number of social media accounts has shown that ISIS and other rebel groups such as the Free Syrian Army have Facebook and Twitter accounts already transmitting a copious quantity of information regarding the conflict in Syria. The messages posted on social media, and the virulence with which these spread, have been fully aligned to ISIS' creed in its mission, beliefs, practical information on how to join the group and what the fundamental objectives of the militia are (Richards 2016:205).

ISIS' 'PR' strategy had a dual purpose: whilst gaining territory through warfare, extreme violence and displacements, it used a sophisticated PR strategy mostly based on social media use and engagement. This strategy was directed towards two different audiences with two opposing goals – to recruit fighters and intimidate the international community (Weiss and Hassan 2015).

ISIS gained significant advantages from this strategic use of propaganda in contrast to other terrorist groups: through the use of social media, ISIS was not reliant on the classical mainstream media and news agencies (Jones 2015), compared to the terrorist organisations of the past who would only be able to attract public attention through the reports of the mainstream media.

With the use of social media as a propagandistic tool, ISIS had the opportunity to bring its messages directly to a global audience without any of the information being filtered through the lens of Western media. Since it still can post images with various commentaries attached, Christopher Jones (2015) argues that it can create, own and manage the global public image of the Islamic State.

ISIS is quite sophisticated in its use of social media manipulation and propaganda. The group's ideological wing, supported by its Media Council, disseminates religious edicts, battlefield updates and specific threats through official platforms that can reach sympathizers and new audiences via social media (Jones 2015). In particular, shortly after it renamed itself the Islamic State of Iraq in 2006, ISIS established the al-Furqan Institute for Media Production, which produced film DVDs, posters and internet-related propaganda products (Gerges 2016). The ISIS Media Center also targeted a Western audience and produced materials in English, German, Russian and French. Other official ISIS internet platforms, namely Mu'assassat al-Furqan, produced and released videos across social media, such as those showing the beheadings of James Foley, Steven Sotloff and David Haines (Rogers 2016).

ISIS has used both Archive.org's forums and Justpaste.it, a website where anyone can post messages and images anonymously, and it has even created its own application, 'Dawn of Glad Tidings', to efficiently tweet messages to its followers (Wanlund 2015). A United Nations (UN) security report shows that hundreds of supporters have subscribed to the information services provided by ISIS via its

'Dawn of Glad Tidings' application. By hijacking the trending topics, especially the political ones, ISIS' message could reach anyone in a short time, and their objective for spreading their propaganda was met (Erelle 2015).

ISIS' social media networks have remained flexible and resilient in the face of efforts to dismantle them, although it is becoming harder to maintain extremist social media profiles undetected. In August 2014, Twitter administrators shut down a number of ISIS-associated accounts (Neumann 2016), with ISIS recreating and publicising new accounts the following day (US Department of State 2017).

This cat-and-mouse pattern is still ongoing. ISIS can quickly spread information about new accounts by either providing backup account information in its profiles or by using accounts that have not been shut down. The conflict between ISIS and Twitter has even led to ISIS directly threatening one of Twitter's founders (Kosoff 2016). The group has attempted to branch out into alternative social media sites, such as Quitter, Friendica, VK and Diaspora; Quitter and VK, nevertheless, immediately worked to remove ISIS' presence from their platforms (US Department of State 2017).

ISIS' online recruitment drive penetrated as far as Australia, having led in 2015 to the apprehension of two teenage boys at Sydney Airport on their way to Syria: 'The boys had become radicalised jihadists over the Internet and officials said their parents were "as shocked as any of us would be" when they were told their children planned to join the violent terrorist group' (Clarke-Billings 2015). The Australian authorities have indicated that almost 100 Australian nationals left the country to join ISIS: 'The latest figures come as an Australian ISIS fighter in Syria resurfaced on Twitter to mentor prospective jihadists on how to join the death cult' (Scarr and Cordoba 2015).

Similarly, the details of the case of three schoolgirls in London illustrate the power of social media to induce vulnerable young people to join ISIS (Blaker 2015). Investigators believe that Shamima Begum, one of the three London schoolgirls who has recently been stripped of her British citizenship and has given birth to three ISIS-fathered children (Grierson 2019), connected online via Twitter with Aqsa Mahmood. In November 2013, Aqsa Mahmood (now known as Umm Layth) left her own moderate Muslim family and affluent home in Glasgow and made her way to Syria. She was 19 years old at the time. Mahmood's family believed that Aqsa was also likely radicalised online, making contacts online with others who persuaded her to join the extremists in Syria (Engel 2015).

Furthermore, the Indian police recognised that most of their co-nationals' recruitment by ISIS occurs via the internet and consists of females seducing males into the group (Speckhard and Yayla 2017). The American Mohamad Khweis also appeared to have been seduced in this way, marrying his ISIS bride when he arrived in Istanbul and then traveling into ISIS-held territory with her (Speckhard and Yayla 2017).

ISIS' social media machine was, from a pure conceptual point of view, one of the most spectacular ones currently deployed by any organisation – public, private, interest group, non-governmental organisation (NGO) etc. – in the world. ISIS had especially assigned administrators who were fluent in several languages, and those individuals were responsible for ISIS' social media accounts. Female foreign fighters (Speckhard and Yayla 2017) were specifically tasked with the administration of their social media accounts, and they had special offices in Raqqa to carry out their tasks under the control of their emirs.

National governments' communication and engagement efforts to influence their stakeholders and voters into action are very different from the efforts of ISIS' PR apparatus to influence their supporters' base. Firstly, and most obviously, when regulators seek to ensure businesses comply with a given set of norms, these norms are based on a quite different system of values to the ones underlying the norms propagated by the Islamic State. The international community is focused solely on the current, physical world, whereas ISIS ensures its messaging encompasses the spiritual as well as the physical, the hereafter as well as the here and now. Only by fully acknowledging this dichotomy of engagement and arguments it is possible to understand the coercive power ISIS wielded over those who lived outside the geographic areas under its control (MacDonald 2017).

For instance, new ISIS recruits were – and still are – also called by the name of the country they were originally from, sharing messages and images of their daily life in Syria, portraying the ISIS community as peaceful, methodical and full of determination and resolve (Klausen 2014:21).

One would have thought that the international community, let alone the counterterrorism units of both France and Belgium, would have taken to social media and made various emotion-based appeals to the online communities to counteract ISIS' boasting of their success in the Paris and Brussels attacks. This did not happen – what did happen though was that immediately after the ISIS attacks in Paris and Brussels in 2016, many text-based tweet and images were broadcasted from multiple individual ISIS Twitter accounts to rope in like-minded individuals to praise the violence. To facilitate this kind of participation of ISIS supporters across the world, a coordinated campaign was run through the 'Dawn of Glad Tidings' Twitter application that allowed ISIS to tweet directly onto its users' pages, thus rapidly and widely disseminating its propaganda and enabling effective hashtag campaigns.

During discussions with the author, a series of diplomats who chose to remain anonymous postulated that counterterrorism units may not be in a position to engage with the public across the social media channels for fear that 'their connection to the Government may become apparent and, therefore, the relationship would be counterproductive.' While these arguments may well have merit, unless a dialogue is started and genuine engagement is fostered by the government units themselves, the counternarrative against online extremism will never be complete.

Some of the images used by ISIS were tweeted from between 80–100 user accounts in a matter of minutes (Klausen 2014). The international community was silent on social media, wrongly assuming that mainstream media – newspapers, radios and TVs – were still the most used forms of media by ISIS' target groups. As evidenced in the previous subchapter, they were and are not.

ISIS allowed its followers and potential sympathisers around the world to engage with, and thus become complicit in, the Islamic State's atrocities. One example in this regard was the 'crowdsourcing' of the ways in which the Jordanian pilot captured in January 2015 should be best publicly executed. The degree to which ISIS itself was responsible for the hashtag 'Suggest ways to kill the Jordanian pig' is unclear, but responses received via social media ranged from impaling the pilot to executing him with an axe (Shiloach 2014).

ISIS, as argued in certain intelligence community circles, has built its propagandistic media empire by learning from Al-Qaeda's first attempts to dominate the jihadi narrative on the newly formed social media platforms and making best use of the internet's availability. For instance, one of the killers of fusilier Lee Rigby, Michael Adebowale, had come to the attention of the British security services in 2011 as a result of his interest in online extremist material. Of particular concern was his reading of *Inspire* magazine, produced by Al-Qaeda in the Arabian Peninsula.

An internal Security Service (MI5) assessment of *Inspire* in 2012 described how the magazine, which sought to promote homegrown 'lone actor' attacks, had been read by those involved in 'at least seven out of the ten attacks planned within the U.K. since its first issue [in 2010] and had significantly enhanced the capability of individuals in four of these ten attack plots' (Burke 2015). That is why, early in 2013, Michael Adebolajo described graphically on Facebook what he hoped to do, and, just over a week before the attack on Fusilier Lee Rigby (22 May 2013), he was seen a mile away from the Artillery Barracks in Woolwich manning a stall outside a community centre after Friday prayers and preaching as the congregation dispersed (Kirkpatrick 2014).

'You only die once, why not make it martyrdom?' asked one recruitment video for ISIS. If one were prepared to ignore the systematic rape of the Yazidi women, the massacres of the Shi'a, the torture of the hostages and the execution of medical doctors, ISIS' cause – in the abstract – could be portrayed as a noble one. But there's hardly anything noble when one of the potential martyrs for ISIS' cause, Imran Khwaja, a bodybuilder from Southall, told a friend he needed 'cocoa butter, soap and condoms' for 'the war booty' (Burke 2015).

In the many videos recorded and uploaded, and in their tweets and Facebook posts, ISIS fighters self-consciously posed as champions of the global *umma* ('community' in Arabic, with a meaning that supersedes national identity and defining a common past), fulfilling a duty and a mission of importance and consequence. As they related to a very clear cause which united them all, the international community lacked one – there is still no joint plan to counteract violent extremism online other than shutting down various social media accounts when they become known. There is still no viable strategy in place to counteract ISIS' and other new extremist groups' corporate-style PR strategy and engagement. A reactive style of communication and engagement has its best place in a crisis – but, even for times of crisis, most corporations have a pre-agreed and pre-approved plan of response. With extremist communication, a reactive/response plan comes too late; extremist narratives need to be tackled at grassroots levels by leading the narrative on why joining jihadist extremist movements is not the answer for disgruntled and alienated Muslim youth.

With its newer, fresher, more immediate message, and with its more accessible, less austere tone, ISIS still holds an appeal for a new generation of extremists in a way that Al-Qaeda and other similar extremist groups increasingly appeared to lack. Although the Islamic State never explicitly claimed the Paris Jewish supermarket attack as its own, it did so by implication when Boumeddiene (the attacker) surfaced in Syria a month later and gave an interview to *Dabiq*, ISIS' magazine. In March that year, Boumeddiene was seen again in an ISIS video production entitled 'Blow Up France II' (Burke 2015).

The extensive body of research carried out to date into the online behaviour of far-right extremists has evidenced that the extremist communities that are built on, hosted by and empowered through social media act as a surrogate conventional social network. That fact is hardly surprising since, even for the most arduous ISIS sympathisers, it would be difficult to shout out their beliefs and allegiance to the mission of ISIS publicly – unless this is done in Iraq, Syria or in the final moments before they blow themselves up or allow themselves to get killed in the name of the 'caliphate'.

Just as commercial brands present their customer value proposition to their shareholders, ISIS has successfully managed to position its 'brand' in such a way that its 'offering' brings more additionality than its 'competitors'' brands. Professor Thompson (2016) of the London College of Communication presented the main value proposition pillars of ISIS during a public lecture on extremist narratives in 2016, beginning with their core purpose, that of 'existing and expanding'. The 'caliphate', as far as ISIS leader Abu Bakr Al-Baghdadi and his followers are concerned, is not an afterthought but their ultimate goal. The operations, identity and the strategy of ISIS revolve around communicating this core message: 'we are here, we exist and are expanding – we need you so that we can become greater, holier and stronger than we are.'

ISIS' value proposition, compounded by the phenomenal reach of social media and the inability of social media platforms to completely eradicate ISIS' and other extremist accounts at the same speed they are created, provided its followers with purpose – a purpose which many of them did not believe they have or could ever achieve in their families, communities or wider social groups. ISIS is not just a random fundamentalist, extremist organisation. ISIS is an astute user of socio-psychological principles, one that puts Maslow's 'Theory of Human Motivation' psychological postulates to, one could argue, perfect use.

The international community has failed yet to identify, agree and deploy an inclusive approach and narrative that is powerful enough to sway ISIS' followers and counteract their online dominance. If ISIS is an unconventional extremist organisation that uses corporate PR techniques, tools and strategies to attract and motivate its 'publics', shouldn't the international community build its narrative on the same principles? ISIS was (and still is) fighting a highly unconventional war against the world's democracies, a war that puts to perfect use the tenets of public relations: strategic communication, stakeholder engagement and mapping, influencer relations, content marketing and multi-channel/multistakeholder targeting.

Social media has proved to be the thriving ground for violent and Islamic fundamentalist extremism. No other means of mass communication could have contributed to ISIS' global spread of terror and fundamentalist appeal in the same way that social media platforms did:

> it does not matter if the following coverage on them is negative – say, criticizing the brutality of the group or questioning their religious legitimacy. For the Islamic State, provided it is in accordance with those responsible for their propaganda and transmits the supposed strength and ubiquity of the group, any coverage is good coverage. In this sense, the terrorism of the Islamic State does not end when the bomb is detonated. Instead, it continues for hours, days and weeks, fed by the media.
>
> (Winter 2015)

One could deduce, therefore, that the current status-quo of ISIS' challenge to the international community is far greater in the virtual sphere than it is in Aleppo, Raqqa, Mosul or any other Middle Eastern or Western city. While the joint armed forces of the US, UK, France, Russia, Turkey and Iraq are making significant progress on the ground, the same cannot be said about their progress online.

3

A FAILURE IN PUBLIC ENGAGEMENT

The Organisation for Economic Co-operation and Development (OECD) published a report in 2015 entitled 'Reaching Maturity in Government Use of Social Media' (2015). The report is filled with very interesting and actionable insights, but the one thing that stands out dramatically for the purpose of this book is some authoritarian governments' shift towards unconventional forms of communication, in particular Saudi Arabia's and Afghanistan's. This dramatic shift could be ascribed to their citizens' and international community's need to stay informed and be informed regardless of the government's actual appetite for public engagement. Posting information and various content on social media does not represent engagement unless there is a dialogue component to it. However, even the fact that today, four years on since that OECD report, more and more governments and their departments are present (and engaging, to some extent) on social media is testament to the power of this still untapped platform for mass influence and change.

As demonstrated throughout the previous chapters of this book, the rise of the internet has influenced the negative and the positive behaviours of modern society. It is also through social media and the internet that activist groups have led to democratic uprisings such as those witnessed in Tunisia and Egypt during the Arab Spring. What the internet has abundantly demonstrated was that democracy can be facilitated and brought by it.

There are many initiatives and strategies governments all over the world could take to reduce the online reach and power of terrorist and extremist, faith-based groups like ISIS. These initiatives should include more collaboration with and cooperation from the social media platform providers themselves. The research presented throughout this book finds that diplomatic resolutions in ISIS' case have not been as effective as the mass appeals to action that were incited via the internet, such as those evidenced during the Arab Spring when a new government was elected due to popular protests started on social media.

According to Knox Thames (2014), the director of policy and research at the US Commission on International Religious Freedom,

> non-state organizations seek to gain advantages by centering themselves around a particular faith tradition, using both licit and dark networks to advance their goals. These groups seek to exacerbate societal cleavages or prejudices to advance their religio-political agenda. Wrapping themselves in the flag of piety allows them to justify their heinous acts as divinely inspired, while trying to ingratiate themselves within a larger faith community. The wider world views them as terrorists, but they see themselves as faith-based organizations.

ISIS made intelligent use of social networks to deliver focused messages to specific target audiences, namely Muslim communities in Western and Asian countries. Until now, ISIS' PR strategy has succeeded in positioning the organisation as the main enemy of the West, branding it as the spearhead in the global jihad struggle, winning support both among Muslim audiences and jihad organisations (Giroux 2014).

An article published by *The Economist* (2015) accurately described the morbid attraction of ISIS:

> although IS's laws are grotesque, other Arab states should take note that its emphasis on quick and firm justice appeals not only to Syrians and Iraqis desperate for order amid chaos. It responds to a burning public need to right decades of perceived wrongs. So does IS's intolerance of corruption within its ranks and its focus, even with limited means, on providing services such as health, education and social welfare. Unlike other Arab states, which tend to be hyper-centralised, IS grants broad powers to local administrators.

Although not the topic of this book, the issue of the weapons easily made available to the ISIS fighters cannot go unmentioned. If the social media communication and engagement strategies of ISIS were not compounded by the devastation it caused on the ground in Iraq and Syria, ISIS' fatal attraction would have resulted in, perhaps, random suicide-bomb attacks in major European cities. But ISIS' fighters captured a significant amount of weapons from Iraqi and Syrian soldiers during the direct confrontations with their governments' forces in 2014–2016. Since the UK is the sixth-largest weaponry exporter in the world (Brown 2018), with the US being the first, Mark Curtis (2003) argues in his *Web of Deceit* that the UK supplies arms to countries known for their abuse of human rights, to those countries on both sides of a conflict, to those countries that have been embargoed by other nation-states and even to the poorest African countries.

While weaponry may represent a lucrative business – UK's exports have increased by 37% compared with the export total during 2008–2012 (McGraw 2018) –

if they fall in the wrong hands, as was the case with ISIS, they would only contribute to the heightening and intensification of the difficulties in reaching a peaceful resolution in a war- and terrorism-torn Middle East. From a visual perspective, given the powerful psychological impact of symbol-laden imagery, the black ISIS flag flying on the M1 Abram tanks in Iraq and Syria (Military Factory 2019) demonstrated to the ISIS' sympathisers and supporters the might and strength of the 'caliphate' and, one could argue, the 'holiness' of its cause – and those images would have never been seen by the entire world if it hadn't been for the penetration and reach of social media.

Social media is based primarily around bringing individual users together and having them exchange information and content. A report by Aistrope (2016:121) shows that social media platforms have played a major role in episodes of contentious political action as they are usually used as a strategy to incite the masses. They are often described as important tools for activists seeking to replace authoritarian regimes and to promote freedom and democracy, and they have been lauded for their democratising potential. On the more positive side, social media platforms have also been extensively used to support human rights campaigns across the developing world and have presented important opportunities for activists in countries with repressive regimes.

Although crucial in furthering the online extremist content and appeal, technological advancements in internet media are not, in and of themselves, enough to have an impact on civil society – there must also be a meaningfully large-enough base of the population willing and able to access these online platforms. Auspiciously, social media's development has coincided with an explosion of internet use and access outside of the developed world. For example, in 2009 the *Jakarta Times* described how online activism assisted in securing the release of two senior officials of the Corruption Eradication Commission that the government had detained (Molaei 2014:50).

Similarly, before the 2011 revolution, Tunisia's repressive government was supported by the United States and France. When social unrest occurred, it barely made the headlines. The social discontent that had been festering for years found both a platform and a voice through social media. The use of social networking and mobile phones' new media-enabling apps elevated the Tunisian voice to a worldwide audience, requiring the international community to respond to pressures brought on by its commitment to protect human rights.

Following the same pattern, the Arab Spring movements, which drew strength and organisation via the virtual sphere, were defined by spontaneity, leaderless movement, diversity and a non-prescribed loose structure, which proved to be their greatest strength (Kamal and Chu 2012). Social media played an essential role in organising people and spreading ideas, as people in these oppressive-regime countries were not allowed to effectively organise in person for anti-regime or social protest activities (Goldman and Schmitt 2016).

As much as social media is a force for good, it can also be used to spread panic, terror, fear and mistrust in the international community's ability to uproot and eradicate online extremism. Twitter and Facebook are the main platforms that have led to ISIS' messages (Gatehouse 2016) dissemination, thus creating an unprecedently strong disciple operation as it was able to reach millions of people worldwide.

Social media made it easier for ISIS to spread terror and recruit new members. Attracting people who have the same beliefs is much easier to achieve through social media platforms as users can remain anonymous and can contact the group and communicate privately (or publicly) on what they would have to do to join the ranks. Social media has become crucial to ISIS' operations because they recruited fighters primarily through social media propaganda, with the main aim of fighting the international community's coalition forces (Schwarzwalder 2015).

The viciousness of ISIS' execution videos, most conspicuously the beheadings of Western journalists by a masked Islamic State terrorist who called himself 'Jihadi John', are indicative of ISIS' reach across cultures, nations and communication platforms – 'Jihadi John' was not a Middle Eastern national; he was a British citizen (Moisi 2016).

If there were just one common denominator among ISIS' sociodemographic characteristics, this would be the young age of its fighters and recruits. They were (and still are) disenfranchised young men who found not only a 'home' in ISIS but, also, a community who understood them and was not quick to pass judgement on them. Reporting this to Maslow's hierarchy of human motivation, one could argue that they found the place where they 'belonged', where they could be themselves and where they could show off and boast about their 'manhood'.

According to Steadman (2015),

> many of these young men are showing off because they want to prove to their friends – some of whom are in the West – that joining ISIS is fun. Like execution or recruitment videos, social media jokes are an exercise in propaganda. No wonder an Isis fighter tweeted: "Praise be to Allah who gave Twitter to Mujahedeen so that they may share their joys and not have to listen to the BBC, al-Arabyia, Al-Jazeera."

There is, therefore, little wonder that the Iraqi government decided to begin blocking social media and video sites across the country after 13 June 2014, at the height of ISIS' social media 'rule' (Mackey 2014).

In 2019, it has become evident that ISIS had, and still has, a surprisingly sophisticated understanding of soft power. During a conversation the author had with a senior director of one of London's largest PR agencies, she was told that there is a rumour that the 'communications director' of ISIS was, actually, a senior PR director who was trained and schooled in the UK. ISIS was, by no means, the most violent extremist and terrorist organisation in modern history, far from it. But, unlike any other, ISIS used a perfectly executed communication and PR strategy to destabilise sovereign governments (Iraq's and Syria's), to incite its followers to destroy remnants (McKernan 2016) of ancient civilisations (Tikrit, Nimrut, Nineveh etc.), to kill women and children in its name and to mobilise not just a physical army but, mostly, a silent yet deadly one that lurks in the depths of the internet and shadows of the social media.

The videos posted on social media by ISIS were meant to be distressing and disturbing – they were meant to not only recruit foreign fighters but also send out an alarming message to the international community and the world of the threat ISIS poses to conventional diplomacy, international relations and multi-governmental bodies (Moisi 2016). When 3,000 years of human civilisation get destroyed and streamed live, when tanks and machine guns are used to mow down UNESCO heritage sites, when the international community is seen to be doing nothing and taking no measures to stop those from happening, no diplomatic dialogue nor conventional forms of official government communication would ever match the force and resonance of ISIS' propaganda.

ISIS has capitalised on the political void created by failed states and by the inability of national governments to address vital political grievances, more specifically the disenfranchisement of youth and marginalisation of certain segments of the Muslim population (Barrett 2014). Driven by a deep dissatisfaction and separation from their own societies, thousands of youth have joined ISIS in the search for an idealistic society that gave them a sense of belonging – if Middle East–based Muslims had joined ISIS, that would have never made the news; it would be, for lack of a better comparison, similar to if one said that Irish nationals or Northern Ireland residents have joined the IRA. What was a shock for the entire world was that, for the first time ever in the history of jihadi extremism, tens of thousands of Westerners – men and women – fled their liberal homes to join ISIS. In this void left by the international community, ISIS has taken advantage of these feelings of disenfranchisement in its recruitment by emphasising the idyllic notion of a utopian Islamic State that addresses Muslim grievances across the globe (Bishop 2016b).

It could therefore be argued that public diplomacy may be a less effective method of bringing about civil change since it is aimed at foreign publics, and strategies for dealing with such publics should be distinguished from the domestic socialisation of diplomacy (Fishman 2007). Nevertheless, separating public affairs that are aimed at domestic audiences from public diplomacy dealing with overseas target groups and diasporas is increasingly at odds with the interconnected realities of global relationships, as poignantly demonstrated by ISIS' case.

The use of cyberspace by jihadi organisations is far from new, but it is poignantly clear that ISIS used the internet and the social media platforms more than any other terrorist organisation (Karaim 2016) ever had. In addition to its technological capabilities, it appears that ISIS' primary innovation in its use of cyber-jihad is its ability to morph from yet another Islamic fundamentalist terrorist organisation into a global brand name that featured prominently in the public discourse in the West as well as in the Muslim world (Wanlund 2015).

Notwithstanding the above, mediation is a familiar theme for international organisations and now, more than ever before, it is one that deserves renewed attention as the domestic and foreign dimensions of engagement with the publics are more connected than ever before (Manero 2015). This is, for instance, the case of the debate on the supposed intercultural split between the West and the Islamic world and is illustrated by the fact that the British Foreign Office now discusses Middle Eastern policy with moderate domestic Muslim organisations (Seip 2016). While this dialogue is a significant step forward, its tangible outputs and outcomes remain to be seen and reflected in a significant drop of the percentages of radicalised British Muslims and, even more, in these efforts' translation into actual calls for unity and understanding, peaceful cohabitation and social exchange between Christian and Muslim communities, calls that need to be made by the unofficial 'influencers' of the various layers and segments of the Muslim community, not just by imams, mullahs or various presidents/chairs of formal Muslim associations.

In addition to the extensive use of social media by its operatives and supporters, ISIS' social media jihad included an abundance of offensive use of the online space for attacks on websites and on those who were not believers in their cause, the so-called 'infidels'. ISIS conducted social media raids in the spirit of the alleged physical raids in which the Prophet Muhammad took part in the seventh century against the infidels (Ibrahim 2015). This was also how the 9/11 attacks on the World Trade Center in New York were referred to by their planners, and various jihadi organisations in Syria use this term to describe their military operations against the Assad regime. Similarly, ISIS' supporters characterise their digital attacks as electronic terrorism. Religion has always been the greatest divider of human society and evolution, and an in-depth discussion on its role in ISIS' online and offline insurgency will be made in the ensuing paragraphs.

There are measures that the international community has taken in the past years to attempt to thwart the constant wave of jihadi electronic terrorism, with the UK's National Cyber Security Centre reporting that, in 2017 alone, 188 cyber-attacks were successfully prevented (Littlefield 2017). At the international community's level, NATO members have signed a Cyber Defence Pledge (NATO 2016) hoping to help combat cyber threats, including those posed by ISIS. Of particular interest is the fact that the UK government has set up a Cyber Security Information Sharing Partnership (National Cyber Security Centre 2016) in 2013, with its only stated purpose being that of 'increasing situational awareness and reducing the impact on UK business'. There is no specific mention that concerted efforts will be made to combat cyber-attacks made by extremist factions, nor that bespoke narratives and strategies will be developed to counteract extremist appeals made on social media, nor that an inclusive dialogue will try to be established between various online publics and government offices.

Despite the various alliances and pledges made by members of the international community to prevent electronic terrorism, ISIS' has successfully managed to take over the social media accounts of the US' Central Command and of some important French websites following the terrorist attack on the *Charlie Hebdo* magazine (Mueller 2016). ISIS supporters hacked into the Twitter and YouTube accounts of the United States Central Command, which is responsible for the US military activity in the Middle East and for coordinating the international coalition attacks against ISIS. After taking over these accounts, hackers replaced the official American emblems with ISIS' black flag and broadcasted messages that were in support of ISIS, its operations and its beliefs (Timreck 2017).

Has the international community forecast such attacks? No, it hasn't. Has the international community grasped the complexity of ISIS' internet knowledge and cyber-crime potential? No, it hasn't. As mentioned elsewhere in this book, while heavy weaponry wars are still proving highly successful, the international community's efforts should also concentrate not only on protecting the nation-states' integrity, welfare and security in physical terms but also on protecting them across the virtual platforms of the internet. ISIS hacking the US Central Command and French websites was meant to be a display of power and might, not necessarily an action which, just like in numerous Hollywood productions, would start a global nuclear war. ISIS wanted to assert its power not just to its supporters and potential recruits but, mostly, to the international community itself – a modern form of jihadi terrorism, far more sophisticated than the usual suicide vest, was born.

Another example of ISIS' incredible online penetration and reach is when ISIS-affiliated hacker groups attacked more than 20,000 French websites in the week following the terrorist attack on *Charlie Hebdo* in Paris (Gitabaki 2015), leading to the servers of these sites collapsing. Those ISIS cyber-attacks were described by a senior French official as unparalleled, being the first time that a country has dealt with a cyber-attack on such an extensive scale from a terrorist organisation.

A popular manual published in 2005 was widely circulated across the cyber-space jihad movement, which includes participating in forums and hacking websites with the aim of participating in the media battle against the West and against the perceived enemies of Islam in the Arab world (Erelle 2015). Currently, the cyber-jihad concept refers mainly to the use of online social networks such as Facebook, Twitter, YouTube and Tumblr (Jones 2015), characterised by a rapid flow of information exchange between individuals. As such, the communication on social media is fundamentally different from that that takes place on the internet – which is hierarchical in nature and based on fixed sites and closed forums (Rogers 2016).

Although the UK has an Office of Cyber Security and Information Assurance (UK Government 2017) responsible for 'engaging with international partners in improving the security of cyberspace and information security', Europol established an Internet Referral Unit (Europol 2015) 'to combat terrorist and violent extremist propaganda' and the US has a Bureau of Counterterrorism and Countering Violent Extremism (US Department of State 2017) to 'promote U.S.

national security by taking a leading role in developing coordinated strategies and approaches to defeat terrorism abroad and securing the counterterrorism cooperation of international partners', separately and jointly they have not managed to eradicate ISIS' appeal and penetration across social media platforms and the internet.

Ninety percent of ISIS' communications over the internet are accomplished through social media (Saif et al. 2016), and ISIS is also considered to be among the most skilled terrorist organisations in the world in terms of its use of social media, especially Twitter and YouTube. ISIS used social media as a weapon of war (Bodine-Baron et al. 2016) to spread propaganda and recruit young Muslim followers: men to serve as fighters and women to wed them and form families in the 'caliphate'.

ISIS followers have established dozens of Facebook and Twitter accounts (Yong Kim et al. 2015). These accounts allowed the group to reach potentially millions of supporters who then could consume and share the group's violent anti-Western ideology. ISIS also used video-sharing websites such as YouTube, where they posted videos of their cruel war methods, such as the beheadings of hostages and the strict eye-for-an-eye form of Sharia law (Gallarati 2016). So far, for instance, the UK government has managed to use the specialised services of a PR agency only to try 'to tackle racist myths perpetuated online by the far right' (Khomami 2017), although, in 2015, the former British prime minister David Cameron announced funding being made available for a counter-extremism strategy (Boffey 2015) 'to build a national network of grassroots organisations to challenge all forms of extremist ideology' and to provide 'social media training and technical assistance to enable small charities to set up websites'.

'Setting up websites' and 'social media training' are almost useless if engagement across the social media platforms is not constantly carried out, conversations in the online space properly conducted and emotions used to elicit a positive response. There is little to no point in setting up a website if no one knows about it or those who do are unlikely to act on the information contained therein. 'Social media training', as so wrongly understood by government organisations and various businesses, is not just about what button to push when and what emoji or fonts to include in the message but, first of all, about ensuring that a real and meaningful dialogue takes place. There is an oversaturation of social platforms today, and grabbing anyone's attention to read a tweet or a Facebook message lost among hundreds of others takes a special set of skills, skills that have very little to do with the technical aspects and a lot with attention-grabbing techniques.

Unlike the feeble government attempts to 'challenge extremist ideology', the ISIS recruiters play on the idyllic notion of a perfect Islamic state that addresses Muslim grievances across the globe (Lesaca 2015) to create an appealing 'brand'. Based on ISIS' social media postings, their main online propaganda messages revolved around seven main themes, which will be discussed in the ensuing paragraphs.

The first theme is the humiliation of the West – ISIS accounts had distinct messages of defaming the West and its operations of suppression of lesser states, including the Islamic ones. This was one of the main themes of ISIS' propaganda messaging, while another is the military nature of the jihad. Some of the social media posts of ISIS' members provided advice on how to join its military, highlighting the power and might ISIS' jihad military had (Cooper 2016). The messages also spoke about the change the jihad military would bring to the world. Other message themes were the transgression of the law by the Western states providing social services within ISIS controlled territory, the hypocrisy of the Muslim leaders and ISIS' ability to administer its conquered territories by providing security and order.

There was a perfectly devised strategy and tactical approach in ISIS' social media engagement. There isn't one in the international community's approach to combat ISIS' influence online – there is only a UN statement (UN News Center 2016) denouncing ISIS' genocide against the Yazidis and a unanimous call on the UN members to fight ISIS (Reuters in New York 2015) and 'to take all necessary measures . . . on the territory under the control of Isil [Isis]'. What appears baffling to the author is the UN's lack of understanding that ISIS' main war against the international community was fought online, not 'on the territory'. If ISIS' calls for recruits had remained unanswered, if their charismatic and fascinating appeals to young Muslims across the world had been completely removed, if the Iraqi army had been properly trained in warfare exercises (so their weapons hadn't fallen so easily into the hands of ISIS fighters), the war on the ground in Iraq and Syria would have been fought by a significantly smaller number of fighters since they would not have had 40,000 additional ones to join them.

Using tech-savvy online recruitment campaigns, underpinned by sophisticated video productions (Paul 2014), ISIS' social media posts were/are primarily targeted at Muslim youth and supporters of Islam (Informed Comment 2014). As evidenced by a statement made by the leader of Al-Qaeda Central in 2005, 'we are in a battle, and more than half of this battle is taking place in the battlefield of the media. We are in a media battle for the heart and minds of our umma' (Hamad 2016).

Unlike ISIS or Al-Qaeda, the international community is not currently fighting for the hearts and minds of its 'umma'. The approach to countering ISIS' extremist narrative online is not unified, centre-led or priority-driven. Forcing social media platforms providers to shut down extremist accounts is laudable, indeed – however, without engaging in a constant online dialogue with the segments of youth which may become exposed to radicalisation, no significant progress will ever be achieved.

For instance, as rightly argued by Drew Harwell (2019) of the *Washington Post* on Twitter,

> the New Zealand mosque massacre that took place on the 14 March 2019 was livestreamed on Facebook, announced on eight channels, reposted on

YouTube, commented about on Reddit, and mirrored around the world before the tech companies could even react.

Even more worrying was the fact that eight hours after the massacre took place, a terrible one and a first in New Zealand's modern history, one in which over 47 people lost their lives, the full footage of it could still be watched on YouTube.

If this still occurs in 2019, five years after ISIS' main livestreamed killings, and the social media platforms providers and the international community still fail to act promptly to remove such horrid images, how likely is it that they were able to act promptly in 2014–2015 and ensure ISIS' related images and videos were taken down? Highly unlikely. Extremism, regardless of it being jihadist or white, is like a wound left to fester for too long, one which can have significant impact on the overall health – in this case, demonstrating to those who have a morbid attraction towards one form of extremism or another that if they go ahead and commit an extremist act, the whole world will be there to watch it, and, 'hopefully', someone else will be inspired to commit similar acts.

Using social media to draw on vulnerable and disenfranchised youth, ISIS attempted to propagate its ideology and build common identifiers with its target audience. Its ability to use various foreign languages and stories of converts and foreign Muslim fighters projected an image of acceptance in which everyone was seemingly united under the banner of Islam regardless of their race, socio-economic barriers or status, physical disability or country of origin (Kates 2016).

In one of his blog posts, Pellerin (2016) shows that the branding statement used by ISIS aimed to make those individuals not already affiliated to it feel as though the organisation was welcoming diverse groups. In one of their Twitter accounts, ISIS claimed that it was a state where 'the Arabs and non-Arabs, the white man and black man, the Easterner and Westerner are all brothers'. These types of propaganda videos tap into the socio-economic grievances of the potential recruits and provide an alternative to economic advancement in their respective communities (Giroux 2014). In plain speak, these powerful statements tell the story of a place where everyone is equal, a place where you are free to wear a hijab if you wish to and no one will judge you, a place where you will be included and not disposed of as an outcast in a refugee camp or in a deprived area of large Western citadels.

While ISIS appears to embrace men and women, Arabs and non-Arabs, black and white, and clearly make them feel 'they have a home', the international community's approach is at the opposite end, with the US president Trump recently banning Muslims from seven countries from entering the US for a period of 90 days and, recently, stating that 'the travel ban into the United States should be far larger, tougher and more specific' (Wilts 2017). Even more worrying is the fact that when one applies for a US visa under the Visa Waiver Program, also known as 'ESTA', the questionnaire one needs to fill in asks, at Question 9, the following: 'Have you travelled to, or been present in Iraq, Syria, Iran, Sudan, Libya, Somalia or Yemen on or after March 1, 2011?'

Not all Muslims are extremists, as not all Christians are peace loving. To single out nationals of seven countries known to have a significant jihadi extremist propensity may not be the right approach since inclusion in a societal system, and acceptance of someone different than we are, does not start by excluding the nationals of that system. And, as it has been so clearly demonstrated by the ISIS attacks carried out across Europe and the US, one does no longer need to 'travel to' a jihadi extremist–rife country – one can be easily influenced and encouraged to commit terrorist acts from the comfort of their chair, thousands of miles away from the conflict zones, by simply using social media.

There is a significant body of literature that attests to the tremendous importance jihadi organisations attribute to the online space, a space which enables them to circumvent the barriers placed before them by various state institutions and security organisations and disseminate their message calling for a violent struggle against the West and the 'infidel' Arab regimes – without interruption, faster and easier than ever before (Benedetto and Tedeschi 2016). Testament to this is ISIS' clever use of social media and excellence at manipulating the online social networks, and a great example in this respect is the fact that, by using the 'Dawn of Glad Tidings' application, ISIS could generate a significant volume of activity across social media platforms greatly exceeding the organisation's true dimensions, thus serving as a force multiplier and an effective medium for psychological warfare (Bloom 2016). The ideology underpinning this strategy was constructed on the premise that the more ISIS was talked about across social media channels, the more recognition it was gaining, and the more it could manipulate the media outlets to receive and broadcast what ISIS wanted them to (Aistrope 2016).

ISIS' jihad 'marketing' was conducted on nearly every possible social media channel, and in so doing, it maximised the possibilities inherent in the online space for disseminating its messages. The two principal effects of this effort were the accelerated recruitment of foreign fighters joining it and the encouragement of terrorist attacks in the West perpetrated by 'lone-wolf' ISIS members (Cribb 2016). The precise number of foreign fighters who have joined ISIS is unknown, but, according to various estimates from the UN, it currently stands at more than 40,000, out of whom approximately 7,000 were Western volunteers, with the highest percentage of ISIS foreign fighters coming from European countries such as the UK, Turkey and France (Cyber Report 2016).

It is therefore paradoxical that the freedoms European nationals enjoy are the same triggers that push them towards signing up to a utopic caliphate, sacrificing their futures and, often, causing irreparable grievance to their families. To put it into perspective and to further emphasise the international community's inability to not only tackle the jihadist movement represented by ISIS but also to build bridges for its disenfranchised population, the number of Western Europeans who joined ISIS exceeded the number of those volunteering to fight against the Soviet Army in Afghanistan in the late 1980s.

One could argue that international governments may find it difficult to engage in constructive dialogue across social media channels with their nationals and citizens of other countries because of a prescriptive, conservative and rather non-committal style of communication. Interesting to note is that the UK's armed forces, namely the Ministry of Defence (MOD), have launched a recruitment campaign for the specialised services of 'philosophers, psychologists and theologians to research new methods of psychological warfare and behavioural manipulation' (Gayle 2019).

Citing Simon Schaffer, a professor of the history and philosophy of science at Cambridge, *The Guardian*, the British daily newspaper that ran with this MOD story in March 2019, mentioned that Cambridge University withdrew its participation in the project because, largely, the reputational risks associated with propaganda and psychological operations' largely unethical issues. It could be argued, though, that touching people's hearts and minds needs not be unethical – it needs to be properly targeted and framed, just as David Landsman PhD OBE argued so beautifully in one of his interviews with *Management Today* in 2014:

> If what you do is out there in the public arena then you need to be part of it, or there will be a vacuum that someone else will fill. My Twitter feed is not full of terribly contentious stuff, but neither can you be too cautious. You have to do it in a way that people want to read.

The International Centre for the Study of Radicalisation and Political Violence, the first global initiative of its kind to combat violent extremism, was not engaging in online conversations with disenfranchised youth, nor was it using emotive images, texts, pictures or chants to try to dissuade potential ISIS recruits to join the Islamic State. What the Centre did is build 'an exhaustive database of Western Islamic State fighters' (Cyber Report 2016), 'ascribing them with data points' and tracking 'approximately 70 women' of Western origin to learn how daily life is in Raqqa. However, in 2019, it does appear that the Centre has an ongoing research project aimed 'to explore how jihadist strategic communication works from a psychological and aesthetic perspective, assessing in particular how it is used to articulate socio-cultural values with a view to radically improving counter-terrorism strategic communication campaigns' (The International Centre for the Study of Radicalisation and Political Violence 2019).

Before ISIS emerged, the Soviet-Afghan conflict was considered to be the conflict that had drawn the largest number of foreign fighters in the second half of the 20th century (Jones 2015). ISIS' activity on social media was ascribed a key role in this record-breaking call to arms, and many of its recruits (as well as those individuals who attempted to join the organisation but were arrested by the security agencies of various countries prior to enlisting) attest that ISIS content on social media affected their decision to join its ranks. There is no evidence whatsoever that was identified during the research for this book indicating that individuals were dissuaded from joining ISIS by the online counternarrative of their own governments or of the international community.

Contrary to the current body of evidence, the United Nations Security Council (UNSC) argues that social media should not be credited with an exclusive role in ISIS' process of radicalisation and recruitment. Furthermore, Christopher Jones (2015) argues that the battlefield successes of ISIS constitute a more significant factor in the decision to join its ranks than the organisation's effective use of social media, the author attributing the flow of foreign fighters to poorly policed borders and the ease of travel to Syria.

An e-book published by ISIS entitled *Migration to the Islamic State* detailed how to reach the caliphate territories and what the prospective traveller should pack. Sharing such information on the internet and engaging on social media with its sympathisers provided those who had and still have an interest in ISIS with an easy interaction with the group (Gambhir 2016) since, in addition to facilitating the flow of foreign fighters, ISIS' social media strategy encouraged the phenomenon of lone wolves who, inspired by the organisation but with no official affiliation to it per se, perpetrated terrorist attacks in the West. For example, the terrorist attacks in Sydney, Paris, Nice, London and Copenhagen were perpetrated by individuals who were influenced by ISIS and used its flag without being formally affiliated with the organisation (Rogers 2016). This circumstance of having individuals committing terrorist acts in the name of an organisation whose 'official' members they are not should serve as an additional reason for the international community to own the narrative on social media.

There is a school of thought and best practice in PR and strategic communication that recommends that for every communication action there should be a communication response. As it can be seen from the paragraph above and others earlier, ISIS did publish an e-book, created an app, had its own magazines etc. How did the national governments or international community respond to those communication outputs? They didn't – if one searches online the phrase 'don't join ISIS', the only resource that appears on the first page of Google's search result is a website called 'openyoureyes.com'. The website does not disclose who it is owned by or who is behind it, only that they work 'with young people, activists, bloggers, and filmmakers to raise our voices against ISIS', and their mission is 'to get involved and raise your voice' because 'together we will crush ISIS propaganda' (OpenYourEyes.com 2019).

This website represents a very good step forward, only it comes almost four years too late. The most daunting fact is that after having combed through pages 1–20 of the Google search results mentioned above (as of 17 March 2019), the only resource found was the one mentioned above, that of OpenYourEyes.com. Have any e-books been published online by governments or various international coalitions? Have any apps been produced? Have any emotion-filled and purpose-led messages been included in a 'message' board for the Muslim communities? Are regular resources published in print (multilingual) and shared with Muslim mosques and their imams so that they can offer them to their congregations? Are Christian spiritual leaders invited to address Muslims during their prayers, emphasizing what humanity has more in common than apart?

ISIS saw the terrorist attacks carried out by its lone wolves across the West as a success and took great pride in announcing the world about them. ISIS also released video clips praising Omar el-Hussein, the terrorist responsible for the Copenhagen attacks, and called for additional terrorist attacks by lone wolves (Melki and Jabado 2016). Lone wolf attacks, which are, for the most part, perpetrated with no early warning, allow ISIS to operate outside the Middle East through sympathetic operatives and supporters. ISIS' message to Muslims in the West is thus very clear: even if they cannot immigrate to the territory of the Islamic State and join its ranks, perpetrating terrorist attacks and attacking Western symbols in their countries constitute a worthy alternative and a highly praised initiative.

ISIS' uncanny ability to make the best of what social media can provide inspired acts of terrorism, conveyed remote instructions with respect to the preferred targets without the need for physical communication between the perpetrators and ISIS operatives, and conferred legitimacy to ISIS' cause following the success of the perpetrator's attack. The lone wolf occurrence, which has already materialised several times in the recent past, currently poses a significant threat to Western countries and to the international community, particularly given that the terrorist and extremist message dissemination still thrives across the social media (Nance 2016).

The combination between frequent messages on social media and images and video clips of carnage created a deterring and frightening effect for the international community. It also succeeded to negatively influence the morale of ISIS' adversaries (McCabe 2016:140). A clear example of this can be seen prior to ISIS' takeover of Mosul, the second-largest city in Iraq, in early June 2014. The organisation's takeover of the city was considered by international security analysts to be impossible, as the ISIS fighters who took part in the fighting were no more than 1,000 against thousands of Iraqi soldiers armed with American weapons and equipment defending Mosul.

However, despite the odds looking to be against ISIS, the militants managed to take over the city after four days of fighting, while many Iraqi soldiers shed their uniforms and tried to assimilate into the civilian population in an attempt to evade their attackers (Accad 2015). Alongside the structural weaknesses of the Iraqi military, the cunning use that ISIS made of social media is alleged to have had a significant role in this success. Looking at the situations that preceded the takeover of Mosul and the fighting for it, it was clear that social media played a vital part in this war, especially in light of commanders and fighters in the Iraqi forces attesting that ISIS had begun a social media campaign nearly a year before the conquest of the city in order to show how they kill those who oppose them and take their children and kill them, too (Davis 2014). Fear of what may happen trumped the Iraqi army's will to see what would actually happen had it continued fighting.

ISIS provided its enemies with advance warning of what would happen to them and their families should they be caught – torture, beheadings, rapes and murders. These techniques deployed by ISIS are not new; only their form of 'presentation' is. Such psychological terrorising techniques have been largely used in the past, at least from the First World War onwards, if not before (perhaps even before the rise of the Roman Empire and the Inquisition). But, unlike the rudimentary means of mass communication of almost two centuries ago, ISIS had the massive advantage of using the mass message amplification provided by the social media platforms. Has the international community provided ISIS with an advance warning of what faith would await its fighters should they be caught? No. Has the international community provided any explicit materials as to what 'punishment' would look like, other than various public statements and unanimous decisions of the UN Council? No. The question for the author, as well as for many other academics and practitioners in the field of PR and strategic communication is clear: why not?

ISIS was using social media to enhance its psychological warfare, and, as evidenced in this book, it was obviously successful (McCabe 2016:140). To leverage all its opportunities of recruitment, ISIS used social media as a marketing tool and, for this purpose, implemented a strategy tailored to individual target audiences. As Jones (2015) rightly argued, the opportunities currently available to terrorist organisations recruiters for communicating with young people in the wake of the popularity of social media are unique and bigger than ever in the history of terrorism.

As further evidence to ISIS' rather unprecedented approach to treating jihad as the objective of a very carefully targeted PR strategy, the messages it disseminated across the social media platforms differed between men and women, using symbols and images that were tailored to their respective target audiences. For young men, ISIS used images from the days of early Islam of knights on horseback, epic battles and glory on the battlefield, images which were displayed throughout the publications of the organisation and in its high-quality video clips. For women, on the other hand, the marketing of the messages used emotionally loaded images, such as pictures of kittens (prominent on the Twitter account 'ISILCats') and other soft pictures that women could psychologically relate to, such as flowers (Jones 2015).

Perhaps the only other pre-21st-century social experiment that came close to that of ISIS today was Hitler's Nazism. There was also a striking similarity between the way in which Nazi Germany educated and taught its young and the way ISIS did it: the former used to perceive its youth as a vehicle for change and as the New Reich's propaganda vehicle – and the latter allowed its teachers to teach the children only concepts and 'truths' carefully crafted in strict observance of Sharia law.

Despite the fact that, for the international community and democratic nations, Islam has not been associated with a female-friendly environment, ISIS also disseminated messages of female empowerment with photos of armed operatives in the al-Khansaa Brigade – the women-only armed unit of ISIS named after a female Muslim poet from the time of the Prophet Muhammad. The subliminal message of that approach is blatantly clear: in ISIS, women are independent, carry weapons and are capable of defending themselves (Rogers 2016).

The underpinning message is that in a fundamentalist organisation such as ISIS, women can gain protection, status and empowerment that they could not attain in the traditional society in the Arab world or even in the liberal West. This media entrapment strategy attracted numerous young girls and women to join ISIS and ensured that the 'branding' of the terrorist group was suitable to all those who were interested in joining it (Rogers 2016). Needless to say, the main actors of the international community – the US and the UK – have only very recently begun to broadcast and clearly promulgate the message that their respective armed forces allow Muslim women to fight alongside men and fend for themselves while still allowing them to attend daily prayers, although wearing a hijab during operational activities is still not allowed (Hookham 2018).

Conducting terrorist operations is a resource-rigorous activity that requires terrorist groups to continually seek out new recruits to replace the individuals lost to fighting and to other operations that may claim their lives (Schwarzwalder 2015). Social media has led to ISIS finding and persuading youth and even women to join them, allowing them to meet one of their key objectives, namely to have enough human resources to operate efficiently (Investigative Project on Terrorism 2016). With the majority of ISIS members dying willingly during suicide bombings, the organisation needed new recruits to expand its operations. Over the past four years, both ISIS and Al-Qaeda have turned to the internet as a recruitment tool, presenting their ideology in an often 'slick' packaging (Moore 2015). Indeed, ISIS members and their supporters could be found using a variety of social media apps and file-sharing platforms, from Facebook and Twitter to YouTube (Kamal and Chu 2012). Within these online spaces, ISIS and Al-Qaeda provided their followers and sympathisers access to, among others, music videos and online articles with messages targeting directly disaffected Muslim youth (Just Security 2015).

What these communications typically had in common is the manner in which they presented jihad – a cool way of expressing dissatisfaction with the powerful elite (Iosifidis and Wheeler 2016). One study undertaken among the American ISIS recruits found that the individuals who got recruited have certain socio-psychological and anthropological characteristics: they were typically confused young people searching to define themselves and gain a sense of purpose (Just Security 2015). Therefore, ISIS' ability to turn the new recruits to violence was rooted in what each of those individuals actually sought (Lia 2015): purpose and meaning.

Some of the elements the new recruits sought and still seek were vengeance, thrill and/or a sense of belonging. By analysing the nature of the people who become easily recruited, it was observed that these usually have damaged personalities brought on by their upbringing or social circles (Turley 2014). For example, a youth who has been shunned by his peers for his ethnic or religious background may have bottled emotions and hatred towards his peers (Mahood &

Rane). When an opportunity to join ISIS came along, further emphasised by its powerful and resonating messages, it may have easily swayed the youth to join the group based on his/her peer-group experiences (Manor 2015).

Revenge seekers need an outlet for their frustration, status seekers need recognition, identity seekers need a group to join and thrill seekers need adventure (Solomon 2016). ISIS' masterfully crafted media content was pitched at audiences in ways that exploited these longings. Videos on YouTube emphasised romantic notions of brotherhood, revolution and sacrifice in pursuit of an Islamist utopia (Barrow 2015). Photos of dead 'martyrs' and children wounded in drone strikes were used as propagandistic materials to represent jihad as a defensive strategy against Western, Saudi and other state powers – messages that were ubiquitous across Twitter-land and other social media sites.

The interactivity of social media chatrooms, social networking sites, message boards, video hosting sites, blogs and e-mails shaped the lines between readership and authorship that previous generations of terrorists and sympathisers encountered with pamphlets, newspapers and newsletters. This blurring possibly encourages people who interact in such forums to more easily see themselves as part of broader jihadist movements and not just casual readers or online spectators. They may eventually engage in more substantive activity, such as actual propagandising, financial support or joining a terrorist network (Garcia and Al-Khalifa 2013:66), and the international community's efforts to prevent this from happening appeared to be unsuccessful at best and non-existent at worst.

While much of this propagandising still involves the rather standard techniques noted previously of exploiting grievances, demonising targets or promoting a culture of martyrdom, it also regularly entails efforts directly aimed at making jihad look appealing to younger audiences (Homeland Security Digital Library 2016). Aside from posting romanticised or hyper-masculine images of ISIS fighters to portray jihad as an amazing feat, pro-jihadist supporters employed another communication strategy now commonly found within and across various internet subcultures (Hall 2015): political jamming. Political jamming is the style in which ISIS penetrated the popular culture through social media and the news with a view to gain the audience's attention and to shift messages from their intended meanings in order to spread their propaganda (Altheide 2016).

The evidence against the international community's ability to counteract extremism, to build communities of purpose and values, to motivate a culture of inclusivity and to make the best use of the most penetrating information platforms of the 21st century – social media channels – is disheartening. The gap between the voice of the people and the agendas of the political elites is widening, and there is an abundance of opportunity for individual governments and the international community to engage with the young generation where it can be regularly found: on social media.

Before ISIS' rise to global 'fame', social media had never been considered a direct threat to a nation's sovereignty, to peace, to a friendly multi-religious cohabitation and to freedom of expression – today, it is.

4

DISCUSSION AND ANALYSIS

Being characterised by intimidation through acts of cruelty and violence, with abductions, assassinations, executions and sheer violence among its principal means of manifestation, terrorism has been present throughout over two millennia of mankind's history; its forms and actions are varied and vary according to the final objectives it was and is aiming to achieve.

One could argue that terrorism is a product exclusively pertaining to modern times – it is not. Under various forms, it has been practiced throughout history, affecting most nations, leading to reprobate acts that had dire consequences for the ordinary course of inter-human and international relations.

Today, there are different forms of terrorism, some targeted towards the international community or against the social and political regimes within states. Such acts of violence, as demonstrated elsewhere in this book and as corroborated by the recent waves of terrorist attacks in Europe, the Middle East and Asia, jeopardise international relations and represent a direct threat to the global peace process. Moreover, according to their intensity and impact, they can worsen bilateral relations between states and have negative consequences for the internal climate of any nation-state. Terrorism seems to be unstoppable by any one state's legislation, governance and armed forces – its lawlessness and non-abidance by the conventional legal and societal rules make it difficult to address, prevent and counteract.

The rise of a new Sunni extremist group in the Middle East has become the most significant security threat in the last decades not just for the Middle East but also for the Western civilisation. Finding its roots in the centuries-old conflict and instability in the region, the Islamic State of Iraq and Syria (ISIS), founded by Al-Qaeda's regional affiliate in the Levant, became an independent entity when Ayman al-Zawahiri (Al-Qaeda's leader) disavowed the group in the beginning of 2014. Shortly after, ISIS caught the attention of the Western world with its quick, unprecedented territorial wins beyond Syria and rapid advances into Iraq and even Lebanon. In its path, ISIS left nothing but desolation, terror, horror and human despair, while, ahead of it, the promise and glory of a long-awaited 'caliphate' was becoming more realistic, body after body and mile after mile.

In an age of multi-channel and constant social media communication, terrorism is far from being eradicated. Social media has widened the gap between terrorist factions, international organisations and nation-states even further due to, especially, the dichotomy of engagement styles with population masses. Terrorists know their target publics, understand their subliminal psychological drivers and masterfully use various communication tools and techniques to attract followers, supporters and recruits. Governments and international organisations, generally reliant on a prescriptive and politically fuelled rhetoric, are finding it difficult to engage in online discussions in an appealing and emotional manner – an online presence, as evidenced in the chapter 'A failure in public engagement' in this book, does not automatically translate into a bilateral dialogue between governments and people; it only portrays an online presence which, in the case of international organisations, is nothing more and nothing less than a unilateral dialogue (or, better still, monologue), not an online conversation.

'High power-distance cultures', as defined by Hofstede, Hofstede and Minkov (2010), are by no means open to civil activities or any other liberties of expression or manifestation: 'high power-distance is a term defining people belonging to a specific culture and how they view power relationships – superior/ subordinate relationships – between people, including the degree that people not in power accept that power is spread unequally.' For the current populations of such countries – the Middle East being the strongest foothold of highly restrictive and high power-distance national cultures – the rise and constant expansion of social media have provided them with means of communication, engagement and dialogue which, otherwise, they would not have had an easy access to.

China boasts one of the oldest and strongest high-power distance cultures, having on its payroll a series of informal agents: bloggers and activists operating online on behalf of the Chinese government (King, Pan and Roberts 2017). They send spam e-mails, issue false information and defame the Chinese government's opponents. There are also times when the political leaders of problematic states use the internet as a propagandistic platform. These are the cases of the former Russian president, Dimitri Medvedev, avid blogger and savvy user of social networks, and Hugo Chavez, a very active Twitter user. Thus, it could be argued that the internet becomes yet another instrument by which political power exercises its dominance, imposes its point of view and marginalises any critical views, just as it allows extremist views to flourish.

The resonance of history is important in understanding the dynamics of the region where ISIS had its stronghold. The United Arab Emirates is the centre of the Sunni system and feeling under severe threat by ISIS. Fourteen years ago (2005), Al-Qaeda initiated an attack in the Kingdom of Saudi Arabia (KSA) that was aimed to start a Sunni insurgence. Now, ISIS is targeting the Shi'a Muslims in the KSA, with Bahrain being the stronghold of influential ISIS ideologists (Hassan 2016). It is therefore obvious that KSA will continue to be faced with ideological challenges since KSA was intended to be a territorial state, not a religious one, as per the Saudi King Abdul Aziz's Decree of 1924. The Sunni and Shi'a divide is so wide and complex, and so rooted in Islam's history, that it seems hardly conceivable that the religion that once created both strands of 'Islam' will also be the one that would unite them back – Christian Catholics and Orthodox are still deeply divided, for instance, and Ireland and Northern Ireland represent an example of a fragile solution to a deep religious animosity.

The global threat of jihadi terrorism has rocketed due to the rise and success of ISIS, this hybrid organisation that combines the elements of a proto-state, a millenarian cult, an organised crime ring and an insurgent army led by highly skilled former Baathist military and intelligence personnel (Stern 2015). ISIS' ultimate goal is that of destabilising and, eventually, taking over Saudi Arabia – if this were to happen, the consequences not only for the GCC region but for the world would be profound.

The globalisation of the religious conflicts gave rise to the dispute of whether the secularisation exists or not as a characteristic of the modern society. The concept of secularisation oscillates between secularisation viewed as a forward-moving front and secularisation as a tiring war between the movements for and against it. Irrespective of its form, as long as modernism builds a new experience of existence, the secular and religious become subject to a complementary 'dialectic' governing the new sensitivities, identities and political-economic projects.

As exemplified in the previous chapters of this book, ISIS poses significant challenges to the international community. These challenges are not only related to its ability to be an 'unusual' terrorist organisation in terms of its recruitment practices and incitement to action but, also, in terms of its ability to play on the political discourse of the international community.

ISIS made sure it used any suitable political news to shift the meaning of those messages for its own purpose. A clear example in this regard was the recent ban of immigrants by the US president from countries such as Syria and Iraq. As can be expected, this type of news only fuels further outrage among the already disenfranchised Muslim youth, and ISIS ensured it built on the momentum created to spread its propagandistic agenda (Hall 2015).

A method and technique long used by counter-culture and anti-consumer groups to spread political and anti-consumer messages, ISIS made the best use of culture jamming – a form of cultural politics that allows jammers to confront the image of the society by undermining the image by way of image itself (Hall 2015), thus imploding its logic and presenting the viewer with an alternate, often ironic or satirical meaning. A classic example of this technique is the use of the 'Yes, we can' poster used during former US president Barack Obama's re-election campaign and the shifting of the message to read 'Yes, America will take your freedom and rights'. This technique was famously used by ISIS in spreading its messages, as there were many social media users who only believed in what the group had to say (Gibson and Lando 2016).

ISIS used both political and cultural jamming to create a disruption in public behaviour (Spencer 2015), using culture jamming to alter the behaviours of its news consumers (Klein 2017) and political jamming to change individual and group attitudes towards public policy, hoping that it would spur changes to government practices or regimes, as it did in Syria, and/or influence global social change (Wood 2015), such as destabilising political regimes in the Western countries its supporters committed terrorist attack in.

As mentioned elsewhere in this book, both social media platforms and Western governments alike have attempted to curb ISIS' social media penetration to ensure that its messages – either political or cultural – are not easily accessible to those who may be swayed to join ISIS in some way. As exemplified in the previous chapter of this book – 'A failure in public engagement' – such attempts largely failed: while social media providers suspended user accounts that violated their terms of service, these did not appear to engage in internet protocol blocking or other measures that made re-joining that social media platform difficult (Van Buren 2016). Consequently, individuals whose accounts were suspended re-joined the platform within hours and resumed tweeting until reported again.

As an example in this regard, in 2015 alone ISIS' supporters were using at least 55,000 Twitter accounts and more than 30,000 Facebook accounts (Atwan 2015); their social media usage and penetration were determined by the kind of messages the account holders were using and the words they were using in their messages. To identify such accounts, search algorithms for the words used in each account were being used, particularly words such as 'suicide', 'blast', 'bomb', 'kill', 'Allah' and 'infidel' being some of the known words to look for when searching for accounts belonging to ISIS or other jihadi groups (Lia 2015). Three-quarters of ISIS' online account-holders/supporters listed Arabic as their first language, but nearly one in five listed English. These 'English-native' accounts also had a higher-than-average numbers of followers, more than 1,000 each, and a higher-than-average number of messages sent out.

Furthermore, in February 2016, a UN report on ISIS' social media use explained that more than 90,000 pro-ISIS messages were posted on social media (Klein 2017). While the exact source of that figure remains unclear, the UNSC research has presented data that points to a much higher number. According to the research done by the UN, there could have been as many as 300,000 pro-ISIS tweets and Facebook messages sent daily, while, as it will be seen later in this chapter, the US' foremost authority in combating online extremism had only succeeded in sending 5,000 tweets in a year.

As evidenced throughout this book, the internet and social media networks were the chief means of spreading ISIS' philosophy and political messages, as well as the main means of recruiting foreign volunteers and attracting financing. ISIS used several online platforms, such as the 'al-Furqan Institute for Public Relations Production', which served as the official media arm of ISIS and its leaders, and the 'al-Athzam Agency for Media Production'. Additionally, there were other 'media houses' tasked with spreading ISIS' messages on social media and creating strategies that were directed towards the recruitment of more disciples (Jackson 2015). Another media arm of ISIS' almost perfectly functioning PR machine was the one behind its website – the 'Life Media Centre' – whose messages mainly targeted the Western audience (Johnson et al. 2016).

'The Life Media Centre' contained a great deal of material about ISIS' history, mission and vision, including speeches and video clips translated into more than seven languages, and it combined diverse content with new video clips and subtitles for earlier video clips in addition to articles, news reports and translations of jihadi material (Jackson 2015).

ISIS' website was of high quality, and it was most likely designed by a web development team experienced in producing material for a Western audience (Farwell 2014). ISIS' website was specifically designed to target foreign nationals, its core communication and engagement strategy being to match the right kind of media and message to the targeted audience, and use that media and messaging content to disseminate their philosophy. All this 'marketing pack' was aimed to show the world the power of ISIS, how dangerous it could be, how it was following the will of Allah and how it was punishing the infidels (Mueller 2016).

In 2014, a short film produced by ISIS showing the beheading of 22 Syrian prisoners was uploaded on the internet and posted on social media. This film was analysed by the Terrorism Research and Analysis Consortium (TRAC) and the Quilliam Foundation, and they both concluded that the film was professionally produced, took many hours of filming and used high-definition cameras and professional editing (Lister 2015). Following its extensive analysis, TRAC concluded that ISIS had a network of social media and media-editing teams all over the world since most of their work was not done haphazardly but by using experts in these areas. Their ability to produce such high-quality and engaging content led TRAC to suspect that some of the international media houses may be unknowingly producing ISIS content for its social media communities (Turley 2014).

This simply shows the importance attributed by ISIS to the use of media channels and its profound understanding of the effect such a film may have on its viewers: generating a feeling of romantic attraction for potential recruits on the one hand, and creating a feeling of terror and dread among Western citizens on the other. The films and documentaries produced by ISIS were not shown to just tell a story; rather, they were shown to exemplify ISIS' modus operandi, its recruitment methods and the induction process for new members (Bodine-Baron 2016). Is the international community attributing the same importance to social media communities, especially those who may be subject to radicalisation by ISIS? Other than ascribing them with 'data points' and collating databases, probably not.

As argued throughout this book, while the group of ISIS supporters may seem small in terms of its number of people, it is considered to be highly dangerous as it is these supporters who are the ones spreading the messages of how and why to join ISIS' jihad. Their influence is much greater in terms of affecting global politics or events, with social media (Lieber and Reiley 2016) and internet penetration and availability playing a key role in terms of ISIS' influence and reach.

One of the main problems the internet and social media have caused the international community is that they are mediums through which terror groups can disseminate their messages easily (Picazo-Vela et al. 2012). The social media users can be located anywhere in the world and are able to spread the message furthering jihad's goals, making the intervention of the international community extremely difficult as it becomes significantly harder to stop the flow of messages to the wider public.

It would be naïve to think that it is just those who are actively involved in Syria's civil war that are influencing the international governments' actions and reactions – those who are sitting at their computers have a significant influence, too. ISIS relies on message disseminators, often Westerners, to spread the group's message, provide religious legitimacy for ISIS' actions and interface, engage and encourage would-be recruits, including answering questions about the life in the 'caliphate'. These disseminators may have never actually been to Syria or Iraq but, nonetheless, they do have an influence over the struggle in that region (Woolf 2016) – they only need a computer and an internet connection, and the damage they can do, collectively and individually, can be catastrophic.

These virtual message dispatchers also act as ISIS supporters, encouraging and providing spiritual guidance to troubled young people who might be open to starting a new life as a foreign fighter in a war-torn land (Goldman and Schmitt 2016). As such, these disseminators often have a greater role than their official one, although they are thousands of miles away from the war-torn regions of Syria, Yemen and Iraq. They can share real-time propaganda photos and videos of equipment, give responses to attacks or provide battlefield information (Feldman 2016).

Sometimes, as emphasized elsewhere in this book, those who have a computer and an internet connection can destabilise a national oppressive regime – as it happened in Tunisia and Egypt – or persuade others to commit terrorist attacks on behalf of the 'great cause of jihad', such as detonating bombs at music concerts (Bataclan Theatre and Manchester Arena), and the role of these disseminators in a conflict such as the one we have witnessed in Syria and Iraq isn't entirely new (Woolf 2016).

During the fighting in Chechnya and Bosnia in the 1990s, extremist groups would distribute videotapes to Muslim communities in the former Yugoslav regions with a view to raise awareness (West at al. 2016:2) of their cause, actions and mission. During the Iraq War, disseminators began spreading messages about the conflict via jihadist forums on the internet and, today, Twitter and other social media platforms have enabled legions of terrorist groups' disseminators to spread much more propaganda at an even faster pace (Petersen 2015). What makes these individuals so dangerous is that it is often the disseminator that lures in potential recruits and, eventually, coaxes a would-be foreign fighter to take that leap and travel to Syria or Yemen and be ready to become a martyr. They embody the PR and marketing of ISIS and other smaller extremist jihadist organisations.

The danger posed by ISIS' disseminators to the international community far supersedes the danger they would have posed had they been using automatic weapons, killing innocent by-standers or wearing a suicide vest and setting it off – they had, and still have, the influence and the power to incite others to join ISIS, incite terror and use others to take innocent lives. Online jihadists are blamed for influencing terrorist attacks that have occurred in the United States, UK, Canada, France and Australia in the last four years. What is different about the Islamic State, and perhaps more dangerous, is that ISIS' senior leaders do not necessarily direct its followers to attack specific targets – something that Al-Qaeda did with the 11 September 2001 terror attacks – they allow(ed) their followers and fighters to choose their own, providing the public spectacle caused by the massacre spreads far and wide across broadcast and social media.

Al-Qaeda, for instance, would have never given anybody an assignment to kill on their behalf until they had been vetted. The Islamic State, however, urged people to travel to join their 'caliphate' and, if they couldn't, they were advised to kill infidels wherever they were and whenever they could and, more specifically, kill someone in uniform: a police officer or a member of the armed forces (Law 2016).

A significant and fundamental difference between other terrorist groups and ISIS is the fact that the rise of social media platforms and various dark-web areas have allowed ISIS to thrive because it inspires and commends violent acts committed by its supporters as opposed to directing these (Law 2016). Al-Qaeda, with the assassination of Oussama bin-Laden, became crippled – there was no leading figure to steer its members and no one to look up to. ISIS, regardless of who may be its leader in the future, will continue to thrive for as long as its supporters find a way to engage with it and get inspiration and encouragement from it. Where do these supporters engage with ISIS? In Iraq or Syria? No, very few travel there – they engage with ISIS online, on social media.

It is particularly because of these reasons presented in the paragraph above that the international community finds it so hard to deal with ISIS' disseminators – they are and can be anywhere across the world, using their influence to cause societal damage by leading the youth of various otherwise peaceful communities to join extremist groups (Law 2016).

Evidence in support of this argument is the example of the American-born, Minneapolis-based jihad supporter with the online name of 'Mujahid'. Well known to law enforcement agencies in the US, Miski (his real surname) exchanged tweets with one of two men who opened fire at a security guard outside a Prophet Muhammad cartoon contest in Garland, Texas, on 3 May 2015. The two perpetrators – Simpson and his co-conspirator, Soofi – were killed. For more than a week before the attack, ISIS' supporters urged fellow extremists to attack the event (Giroux 2014). One of these fellow extremists included Miski, who shared a link to the contest on Twitter on 23 April 2015 and encouraged his followers to go to Garland and cause violence. He tweeted: 'The brothers from the Charlie Hebdo attack did their part. It's time for brothers in the United States to do their part.' Nine followers replied to Miski's tweet publicly, including Simpson. After that, Simpson requested that Miski contacted him privately.

Although that conversation between Simpson and Miski was not public, several minutes before Simpson began shooting at the attendees of Garland cartoon contest, he took to Twitter. He connected the impending attack to the Islamic State, tweeting 'the bro with me and myself have given bay'ah to Amirul Mu'mineem' (Callimachi 2015). The statement meant that the two men had pledged their allegiance to the head of the Islamic State, Abu Bakr al-Baghdadi. Miski then tweeted: 'May Allah accept us as mujahedeen.' The international community is, therefore, threatened by the significant penetration of the extremism disseminators as they are well placed and listened to when it comes to influencing others to join their cause and cause mass casualties (Cyber Report 2016).

As highlighted in the previous chapters of this book, the international community has been attempting to find strategies to reduce the influence terrorist organisations have online. For instance, the US government has tried counterstrategies to combat terror groups' anti-American sentiment online with limited success. In 2005, the US State Department spent USD 15 million on a video campaign featuring Muslims living in the United States. It was derisively nicknamed the 'Happy Muslim campaign', and it was shelved soon after. Additional efforts followed but, as the US slowly rolled out its programs, including those aimed to counter anti-American messaging in chatrooms and to enlist the help of film studios to put together films about anti-terrorism, the terrorist groups were seizing their own opportunities to sway opinions on the internet.

In 2012, UNSC tasked a security committee to collaborate with the US Department of Defense on combating extremist behaviour online, and this led to the establishment of the Center for Strategic Counterterrorism Communications (CSCC), aimed at mitigating the spread of terrorist propaganda on social media platforms (Krona 2014). The idea was to not just try to force the take down of extremist propaganda on the internet but to counter that material online with another view, one against violence, radicalisation and incitement to acts of terror. These actions were also done to prevent the recruitment of youth by extremist organisations (Berger and Perez 2016).

Following the data presented by the CSCC, the UN Security Committee concluded that the Islamic State's victims were predominately Muslims and that the terrorist group was hurting local Sunni tribes and inflicting violence on the local community and, therefore, further action was required. CSCC worked in conjunction with the Central Intelligence Agency (CIA), and employed Urdu, Arabic and Somali speakers to converse on Twitter and Facebook with people who showed signs of being prepared and ready to join the jihadi movement (Karam 2016).

The first efforts made by CSCC included the production of videos mocking Al-Qaeda and defaming the might of its leaders. But, by mid-2013, CSCC's main concern was no longer Al-Qaeda but ISIS. It was becoming obvious that ISIS also had a media centre which, especially at that time, was considered very advanced and highly efficient in dealing with propaganda dissemination. Moreover, as it has become clearer in the latter years, ISIS' 'PR and marketing machine' equipped its fighters with cameras on the battlefield and then used the footage to produce propaganda news reports and feature films (US Department of State 2017).

Also, in 2013, CSCC began a new anti-terrorism campaign program. The program also featured a video called 'Welcome to ISIS Land', which included relevant footage from acts of brutality committed by ISIS. Over the course of 2014, CSCC posted 3,000 anti-ISIS and anti-terrorism tweets and posted 69 anti-ISIS videos online (Bates 2015). Over the course of one day, as highlighted elsewhere in this chapter, the UN reported that ISIS may well send in excess of 300,000 tweets. How could 3,000 tweets per year ever counteract 300,000 tweets per day?

As CSCC tried to counter terror groups' propaganda, it found itself unable to keep up with the sheer volume of tweets and material posted by these. Many argued that the US State Department's efforts put the country in the role of a 'social media punk' (Saif et al. 2016). Supporters of the Center's activities countered that it had suffered because of lack of funding, although it had received between USD 8 million to USD 16 million in funding per year, compared to the USD 180 million per year the Pentagon receives annually to try to sway public opinion and to the USD 650 million spent by the CIA to monitor social media and other open-source intelligence platforms. In 2014, the CSCC leadership changed, and the anti-terrorism campaigns are now all branded as 'terrorism facts' (Patel 2015), their effectiveness, impact and reach being less than those desired.

According to Policy Exchange (Travis 2017), despite the significant ground war wins by the international community in Syria and Iraq, ISIS is believed to produce approximately 100 'new pieces of content every week', with 'online jihadist propaganda attracting more clicks in Britain than in other European country'. In response to this, the British government constantly pressures the social media platforms providers to 'remove extremist content within 2 hours' (Stewart 2017), as the latest data made available by the Home Office indicated that 'ISIS shared over 27,000 links to extremist content in the first five months of 2017' (Stewart 2017). Moreover, similarly to the appeal made by the British prime minister to the social media companies to do their utmost to combat online extremism, the European Council also called 'on social media companies to do whatever is necessary to prevent the spread of terrorist material on the Internet'. (Phys Org 2017).

Although the pledge to join their forces against online extremism made by the British prime minister, Theresa May, and the French president, Emmanuel

Macron, in June 2017 is very welcome (Reuters 2017), this needs to encompass much more than encouraging 'corporations to do more and abide by their social responsibility' and, for sure, much more than 'creating a new legal liability for tech companies if they fail to remove unacceptable content'. The governments themselves, jointly or separately, need to lead the conversation online, thus creating an environment where ISIS' potential recruits feel wanted, appreciated and respected in their own countries, regions and communities. The social media platforms' owners cannot assume the voice of the international community or nation-states, nor can they become involved in a dialogue that speaks to the hearts and minds of disillusioned and disenfranchised people.

ISIS used emotions in its online engagement; the international community used laws and regulations to constrain social media providers. The international community is still very much bound by the very prescriptive rules of 20th-century public engagement; meanwhile ISIS, just as the generation the content of its messages relates to, fully grasps the fact that in the 21st century masses hold conversations online, in the virtual space, not in presidential palaces, conference rooms, the halls of the European Union or those of the United Nations. Tightening the counterterrorism laws and border controls of Western democracies is laudable, just as the UK's newly approved 'Counter-Terrorism and Border Security Act 2019' is (Sajid and Wallace 2019) – but more, much more needs to be done to tackle jihadi extremism, something that no law or act has the power to change: feelings, beliefs and false promises.

5

CONCLUSIONS

Today's diplomacy is as much about the individual who stands for the office as it is about his/her political platform. Post–World War II developments in telecommunications, satellite relay and remote communication have had a far-reaching impact on politics. As it could be seen during Donald Trump's US presidential campaign, as well as in Jeremy Corbyn's election as the leader of UK's Labour Party (and still its leader as of March 2019), elections are now easily swayed by the candidates' image and attitudes rather than by their political pledges and platforms alone. Controversial behaviours and attitudes challenging the accepted rules of public conduct and a 'relaxation' of what is considered diplomatic etiquette are becoming the political equivalent of today's 'authenticity' term.

One could argue that the purpose of diplomatic and international communication has never been stronger than it is today – that of seeking cross-cultural understanding, co-operation and mutual respect. In a globalised era, the opportunity and need to stay in touch and be 'connected' 24/7 are constantly increasing. These emerging tendencies apply not only to private individuals whose number, according to the latest data made available by Hootsuite (2019), has reached almost 3.7 billion internet users, but to governments, too.

The communication means have become agents of socialisation. Their wide accessibility and the dissemination, in a very short period of time, of the newest conquests of culture and civilisation create a profound impact upon various human categories that are all connected to these 'virtual sockets' without which the image of the modern man is no longer conceivable.

The neutral, impersonal formulations of diplomatic messages have been supplemented by evocative and, at times, choreographed visual images that are flooding the media landscape. Technical details, legal texts, articles from treaties and trade agreements are still very pertinent to international relations and diplomacy but, as the international society is becoming more global, the communication between states is also becoming more a stage than a chancery. ISIS took advantage of this 'multinational stage' whose lack of unity against extremist terrorism allowed ISIS to use political jamming tactics on. The void left by the international governments' inability to agree on and find a common language, nuance, message and wider narrative in the global fight against ISIS provided the latter with an almost perfect empty canvas where it could demonstrate to the world its transnational, trans-religious and trans-cultural communication.

The abuses carried out during the French and Bolshevik revolutions, as well as those of the Nazi and communist regimes, are still very much alive in the international collective memory. In such conditions, when the national identity is hard to define in the current European space, no process for the minority integration – be it ethnic or national – can be successful without solutions of harmonisation and cooperation between the two concurrent identities: the identity of the majority, in most cases arrogant and comfortable, and that of the minority, subject to various forms of inequality and discrimination.

The shift that is strongly noticeable due to the dialogue and engagement online is that masses no longer feel attracted or engaged by the 'office' or the political party but by the individuals who represent that office or party. And compared to ISIS' strong attraction and captivating appeal for a certain segment of the Muslim population, the dichotomy between the 'appeal' of the public office and the 'appeal' of a brand (since ISIS is one) is stark. With ISIS it was not, and it is not, about its leader, nor about other individuals holding key positions in the organisation, but about ISIS itself and what it stands for. The same cannot be said about a political party or a certain government office.

Statesmen and diplomats are aware of the underlying and direct meanings of texts and use of various degrees of vocal intonations. Masses are less impressed or attentive to such variations – the direct visual message, the appeal to emotions and the relevance to their needs of safety, shelter and social integration are the ones that matter most. Social media platforms have made the conventional means of diplomatic communication and interaction – from the view point of social mobilisation – more challenging and complex than ever. Diplomats are used to interacting, negotiating and debating issues behind closed doors, in government chambers or over a discreet tête-à-tête – social media conversations, discussions, calls for mobilisation and intervention are changing the international diplomacy landscape in a manner it has never been challenged before.

The complexity of the new communication landscape in international relations is stark: face-to-face communication is still vital and adds gravitas, commitment and intent to bilateral encounters between heads of state. However, to consider that the same approach one would take in a face-to-face meeting should be deployed when addressing an entire nation, let alone a social group vulnerable to be targeted by jihadi extremism, would be highly detrimental to the impact sought. The fate of nations and bilateral relations is no longer dependent on personal encounters between heads of state – it is dependent on the perception the general population and social groups have on such encounters, trade deals or agreements. The political cost of non-compliance, especially in low-power distance (democratic) cultures, is high, and the politicians in office have often been 'punished' by the electorate for not having heeded to the latter's will.

The cyber-utopianism school of thought commits a factual error with regard to internet users. To assume that the online environment exercises only an emancipation effect does not stand up to a minimal reality confrontation. However, it is true that the virtual environment is responsible for accommodating activist networks militating for democracy, in all its forms, and human rights. It is equally true that Facebook, Twitter and other online social platforms have become live platforms where a new global civil society is being created.

Noteworthy is the fact that the greatest majority of the current world's 'evils', such as nationalism, xenophobia, antisemitism, religious intolerance, racism and sexism, have also successfully transitioned into the virtual sphere and have seen a global spread brought on by the online social platforms. Beside the global civil society, the internet also hosts the global civil counter-society, one that is dominated by reaction and resentments. 'Twitter posts do not necessarily remove any national, cultural and religious differences. In reality, these can only make them worse' (Morozov 2012b).

In diplomacy, the use of written and spoken language is critical. However, language has its limitations and it may fail to attract the credibility sought or the attention required. Powerful messages shared and related to by a majority of the target population can reach their desired result – a clear example in this regard is the main message of the UK's 'Leave' campaign spearheaded by prominent figures of the UK's Conservative Party for the 23 June 2016 EU Referendum. In that referendum, 52.5% of the UK voters chose to leave the European Union due to a combination of factors that can be largely ascribed to rhetoric, powerful discourse, body language and human fear. The latter is particularly interesting for the purpose of this book – the message conveyed by the 'Leave' campaign was simple: the migrants are taking the UK citizens' jobs, filling up the schools and placing a massive burden on the local councils.

In addition, the alleged GBP 350 million paid weekly to the EU budget could be used to fund the NHS, a poster on a 'Leave' campaign bus said. Whether the 'Leave' campaign's core messages were genuine and evidence-based is a different matter – what matters is that the 'Leave' supporters ran a campaign targeting the UK's population's hearts and minds: and they won.

The fundamentalist phenomenon appeared at the junction of the contemporary process of globalisation. Composed of two divergent concepts – the ideological orientation towards globalisation and the reactions based on preservation of the current status-quo – the establishment of various fundamentalist concepts overshadows, if not ignores, the history and tradition of specific religions from which these concepts formally stem. The current international appeals for globalisation and inclusion have allowed Islamic fundamentalism to become a global terrorist threat, one that is rapidly expanding beyond its initial Middle Eastern geographical boundaries.

Terrorist groups exploit failed governance in places where governments routinely violate human rights and freedom of expression. Counterterrorism and security can no longer be completely separated from diplomacy, development and education (Stern 2015). Islamic fundamentalism presents its own paradox – while suicide is forbidden by the Qur'an, martyrdom for the cause of jihad is praised and encouraged. The wave of suicide bombings and attacks in the recent years has been partly inspired by the religious belief that there will be rich rewards waiting for the martyrs in the afterlife. Evidenced by the martyrdom videos dedicated to Allah, the frequent jubilation of the families of those who commit suicide and their terrorist group leaders' leaves very little room for doubt that globalisation, the value of human life and multi-party dialogue are redundant discussion points for Islamic fundamentalists.

Terrorism is as old as history, and it includes violent acts committed by nationalist, separatist, anti-colonial and revolutionary movements. Tony Blair (2011) said that 'we will not rest until this evil is driven from the world' – and his statement was regarded by many scholars and security experts as a utopian project which could never be accomplished, and the events of the last decade proved them right.

Social scientists such as Hudson (1999), McCauley and Lawson (2002), Mansdorf and Weinberg (2003), O'Connor (2004) and Zimbardo (2004) concluded that the acts of terrorism could not be ascribed to psycho-pathological problems or personality disorders. The tests carried out on individuals who took part in other types of excessive social violence, as well as on members of terrorist factions, revealed that in certain circumstances individuals who are psychologically sane could commit unnatural acts of violence. Furthermore, according to Hudson (1999:59), the modern terrorist groups have begun to primarily recruit – and ISIS is a perfect example in this regard – individuals with degrees, specialised in communications, information technology, engineering and other sciences.

For instance, Merari (2010) carried out a study to understand the way in which Palestinians would willingly become human bombs, arguing the importance of socialisation in small groups. The extremists were found to recruit young people who were highly patriotic and declared enemies of Israel. They would be invited to discuss their love for the country and their hatred for Israel, leading up to the final test of patriotism and hatred, that of committing suicide by blowing themselves up. To die in the name of Palestine and take at least one Israeli life in the process was considered an honour, one which their families took great pride in – their sons and daughters would become the heroes and heroines of the next generation of suicide bombers.

Religions played, and still do, a significant role in the evolution of radical groups and movements. However, religion was not the bloodiest source of conflict of the 20th century – Lenin, Hitler, Stalin, Mao Zedong and Pol Pot killed millions of people in the name of political manifestos, rejecting religious beliefs and any other concepts of anthropological value. Nevertheless, their ideologies had similar characteristics with various religions, and they took their policies' mission to the level of state-proclaimed 'religion'. In the current globalised society, where an increasing number of governments and international organisations suffer a legitimacy deficit, an increase of the religious discourse's impact on international policy should be expected.

The wars on the ground are defined by geography, clear borders and pre-scribed combat rules of engagement. The internet and social media, on the other hand, have no geography to contend with and no borders. It takes the international community weeks, seldom days, to approve a plane strike or armed troops on the ground in conflict zones. At the opposite end, the internet made it possible to reach millions across the world, in less than a second, with the click of a button.

Technology has made a massive contribution to the way in which people communicate with each other in the 21st century. The printed news – newspapers and magazines – are in steep decline, while the new communication devices, such as smartphones, tablets and wearable technology (smartwatches), are on a sharp increase. One would tend to assume that the less developed nations have less access to technology or to means of mass communication. One would be wrong to assume that: while running water, heat sources or other essential physiological needs may still be difficult to meet in some parts of the globe, technology and interconnectedness take priority: Somalia, for instance, with 43% of its population living below the poverty line, has one of the highest rates of mobile phone use per capita in the world (Thomas 2016).

The internet has not only facilitated an increased communication and interaction among and between a nation's citizens, but it has also encouraged a growing degree of linkage between the civil societies and social movements of different countries. The internet is such a perfect fit for the increasingly transnational nature of political and cultural issues that it has led some scholars to point to the transition towards a more complex, global, information-based society that almost logically shaped the context for new forms of online activism (Rozumski 2015).

Social media is based primarily around bringing individual users together and having exchanges of information and content. Its platforms played a major role in episodes of contentious political action, as they are usually used as a means to incite, lead and influence the masses. They are often described as important tools for activists seeking to replace authoritarian regimes and to promote freedom and democracy, and they have been lauded for their democratising potential. Social media has also been extensively used to support human rights campaigns across the developing world and has presented important opportunities for activists in countries with repressive regimes.

However, despite the clear benefits to national governments and to the international community itself to use all available online means to disseminate a collaborative, peace-inducing and productive suite of messages, there has been little legislative movement taken by the international community and the social media platforms providers to remove or prohibit jihadist propaganda. In 2012, the UN introduced a resolution arguing for the need for website owners that share user-posted videos to take action to remove jihadi and terror groups propaganda. The resolution was referred to the UN's Telecommunications and the Internet subcommittee, but no further action was taken.

One of the negative aspects of the internet and social media platforms, as highlighted throughout this book, is that they have considerably facilitated the extremist organisations' operations. Cutting the terrorists' access to social media platforms will mean that intelligence agencies and their allies will lose out on obtaining actionable intelligence about the groups' whereabouts, upcoming plans and funding sources. There is a trade-off that needs to be carefully considered by the state and non-state actors with regard to what matters most in the online world: privacy, freedom of speech, intelligence gathering or preventing extremism and radicalisation.

The international community and its various 'homegrown' organisations have led the way in online technology innovation, development and reach. American companies, including Facebook, Twitter, Google, YouTube and Instagram, have revolutionised the way communication is consumed across the globe. The new and ever-growing social media platforms have levelled the playing field in underdeveloped countries and have empowered people to expand their knowledge horizons to learn more, spread knowledge, share both true and fake news, establish businesses and increase the information potential.

Social media has also allowed nefarious individuals and organised crime groups to more easily steal personal data, spread hateful speech, broadcast extremist views and incite others to commit violent acts. While governments are trying to track and stop online jihadists, the terrorists so far have been out-pacing and out-sleuthing their law enforcement adversaries (Goldman and Schmitt 2016).

The US has managed to track down and kill Oussama bin Laden and stop any further mass casualty terrorist attacks from reoccurring on US soil. What the US and many other developed countries haven't managed to stop is the spread of extremist ideology. In fact, this has grown, with the former FBI director James Comey (Bedard 2017) arguing that the spread of terrorism in the Middle East represents the very purpose of terrorist organisations' operations. What the international community has not yet succeeded to do nor to achieve is to win the online battle – that is the one front where war must be constantly waged (Brookings and Singer 2016).

The spread of extremist ideology and terrorism started with Al-Qaeda; today it has metastasised, and there are well-organised extremist factions that have sprouted throughout the Middle East and North Africa, from Al-Shabaab in Somalia to terror groups in Yemen and now the Islamic State in Syria and Iraq (Institute for Economics & Peace 2016).

ISIS' recruits have grown up in an age of the internet and are adept at using social media, quickly enhancing their skills alongside advances in technology. These are not individuals to whom the concepts of 'national pride', 'democratic right' and 'civic duty' mean something. Their values are those values they share with their ilk, the dos and don'ts their online community abides by and whose social worth, many times, comes down to the number of followers or likes their acts/messages have gathered.

According to Sir John Jenkins (2016), 'ISIS' teachings and proclamations are no more than a shape-shifting form of Islamic ideologies: ISIS is the latest manifestation of a post-colonial survival in any shape, filled with a sacralised narrative and clear transnationalism, backed by Islamist coups.' Any evidence of Islamic exegesis left behind is destroyed, ISIS being a quasi-state: it has global supporters, and its image is shown as divinely guided due to Abu Bakr Al-Baghdadi's declaring the 'caliphate' in Mosul and quoting Abu Bakr (one of the first followers of Prophet Muhammad) during Islamic State's 'proclamation' ceremony.

Journalist reporting from the Middle East has almost always proved problematic. Many journalists found it really difficult to investigate the news and stories occurring in ISIS-controlled areas in Iraq or Syria. However, there was one source of information that has proved robust and that has been independently verified over the last five years – the ISIS fighters themselves. Their knowledge and savvy use of social media platforms was unprecedented and never seen in any other extremist faction – additionally, the 'PR and social media engagement apparatus' of ISIS operated, one could argue, as well – if not better than – as that of any multinational corporation. ISIS did not use nor court mainstream (traditional) and broadcast media: they were acutely aware of the power held by mass communication, allowing their 'news' and beheading videos to be streamed live and instantly shared across the social media channels because, in 2019, journalists and broadcasters take most of their news content from social media platforms, too (Willnat and Weaver 2018).

ISIS' message of 'statehood' and belonging transcends nationalities, borders and ages: their appeal to arms targets publics and population segments from across the world because, ISIS claims, 'they speak the language of Islam' (Olofinbiyi and Steyn 2018:129). In ISIS' view, the 'state' supersedes the 'nation/country', and the non-adherence to ISIS' values was/is severely punished. Spying on ISIS is the equivalent of spying on the state, and all those who have been caught spying have been brutally punished because they were betraying the 'state', not its ideology, creed or Al-Baghdadi himself.

On 19 August 2014, shortly after 10 pm GMT, a video lasting 4 minutes and 40 seconds appeared on Al-Hayat Media Centre's account on the social networking platform Diaspora. The slick video, entitled 'A Message to America', purported to show the beheading of the American photojournalist James Wright Foley at the hands of a masked ISIS insurgent (Friis 2015). In the video, the ISIS extremist claimed that the execution of Mr. Foley would take place as a retaliatory measure against the air strikes ordered by the US president, Barack Obama, on the 7 August 2014.

On 2 September 2014, a similar yet shorter video was uploaded on the Russian social networking platform vKontakte. Subsequently, three additional videos were released showing the beheadings of the British aid workers David Haines

(13 September 2014) and Alan Henning (3 October 2014), as well as that of the American aid worker Abdul-Rahman Kassig (16 November 2014).

Despite attempted internet and social media censorship, the videos have been widely shared across the available social media platforms, generating what one journalist from the *New York Times* has termed 'a modern guillotine execution spectacle, with YouTube as the town square' (Kozlowska 2014). Senior officials in both the British and American administrations have unsurprisingly acknowledged that the ISIS' beheading videos had a substantial impact on American and British foreign policy (Krauthammer 2014; Chulov 2014; Dowd 2014).

ISIS' Al-Hayat Media Centre became a social media savvy powerhouse identical to the remit and responsibilities falling under the brief of any major advertising agencies, producing anything from one-minute-long 'Mujatweet' videos to hour-long, cinema-type edited films – 'The Flames of War' being one of those, with 'The Flames of War II' being available online, easily found on Google and posted by Jihadology in 2017. The global rise of ISIS' notoriety and savvy use of novel mass-communication channels, as opposed to the traditional ones, also had an immediately measurable impact: a 2015 UN Security Council report concluded that 22,000 foreign fighters have made their way to Iraq and Syria to join the jihadist group. According to US intelligence officials, approximately 3,400 of these new 'recruits' came from Europe and the United States.

ISIS' propaganda machine was unprecedented – superimposed to nation-states' various campaign or election platforms, the comparison doesn't even come close: ISIS catered, one could argue, to all 'tastes': their messages were multilingual; they were accompanied by powerful visual, graphic or audio prompts; and they were often supported by hypnotic chants. Social media – while mostly used by the rest of its 3.5 billion users across the world for peaceful purposes – was employed by ISIS to attract followers, create fear and panic among the masses and portray an image of intangibility. While ISIS had a very clear on-the-ground presence in Iraq and Syria, with various cells spread across Europe, Africa and Central Asia, ISIS' stronghold was and still is the World Wide Web: the place where conventional diplomacy, international relations and diplomatic conventions have failed to gain ground (Wired 2016).

Social media companies are hardly helpless and hamstrung in their abilities to curb extremist material from being posted on their online platforms. Of course, free-speech protection must be considered in any policies or legislation brought forth in this regard. However, therein lies the conundrum: protecting free speech at whatever cost. It takes just one social media user, activist or radicalised individual to identify extremist material on social media, go undetected by intelligence agencies and then commit a terrorist act.

AFTERWORD

Can public relations succeed where conventional diplomacy failed?

International law, diplomacy, interstate co-operation and diplomatic exchanges have reached an unprecedented level after World War II: territories became divided, national borders were redrawn, post-war debts were negotiated in kind or in exchange of political favours and, most importantly for the purpose of this book, a new dawn in diplomatic relations between Europe, the United States and Middle Eastern countries was beginning.

A new industrial revolution emerged, too – one that was not necessarily labour but resource intensive; a revolution which, to be sustained and expanded upon, needed oil – with this 'black gold' (Yergin 2009), a never-seen-before clash of cultural understanding, religious values and societal acceptance occurred: the clash between the humanistic values of Western society and those of Islamic fundamentalism.

The cognitive value and efficiency of any ideology are dependent on the adequate gradual reflection of the social existence, on the objective contradictions thereof and on the influence they gain due to these facts: 'the theory becomes a material force as soon as it engulfs the masses' (Marx and Engles 2015). Ideologies impact other areas of social existence, including the actions that led to their creation, either accelerating or dampening the social development. Also, any ideology's final goal is to serve the requirements of the social action in general and of the political action especially.

The ideological struggle is, together with the political and economic struggles, one of the forms of clashes between social classes and social groups, expressing the opposition or difference of interests between these and, especially, the irreconcilable character of the fundamental interests held by the antagonistic classes – and ISIS stems from such an antagonistic class.

Similar to the Marxist ideological struggle, the 21st century sees a new ideology and severe form of antagonistic social ideological concept emerging –Islamic fundamentalism. While the communist messages and propaganda were revolving around the 'good for all' and an abolition of the class system, the new Middle East–'born' Islamic fundamentalism ideology revolved around the purity of religious beliefs – a class system into its own – and the rise and gains of only those who prove themselves 'worthy'. Without an underlying and decades-old class dissatisfaction related to the economic difficulties and right of expression that has been constantly denied by the ruling classes and royal figures of Middle East, the rise of Al-Qaeda, ISIS, Al-Shabab and others would have never happened or would have only remained on the level of disorganised extremist groups.

To apply a logic reductionism of the internet to a single dynamic – the liberating one – would be to totally ignore the adaptability of the online technologies to different cultural, political and religious contexts. The online tools bring power not just to the oppressed but to the oppressors, too. Far from allowing themselves to be conquered by the liberating internet energies, some authoritarian political regimes have learnt to harness and manipulate them according to their own interests, just as extremist fundamentalist groups have.

The academics concerned with terrorism studies have argued that terrorist organisations and insurgent groups have produced videos with beheadings and explicit atrocities for various reasons, including seeking ransom payments, destabilising transitional states, diminishing the possibility of direct foreign investments in that country/region or arousing fear among the members of the general population (Ubayasiri 2004; Howard-Jones 2016; Campbell 2003). An understanding of the political objectives underpinning each terrorist act may lead to a meaningful dialogue between the disputants and to the eventual resolution of the unequal conflict between a guerrilla terrorist group and regular forces, a battle which is never likely to be solved by military means alone.

Governments, diplomats, politicians and heads of state are not the only ones who are actively trying to engage, sway, persuade and communicate with their followers, subscribers, lobbyists and supporters across the social media platforms – terrorist networks are, too. ISIS has taken the entire world by surprise in terms of its violence, unique recruitment methods and, primarily, in terms of its highly savvy use of social media channels. It can be argued that ISIS is running its 'PR and communication services' with the same attention to detail, consistency and clarity of message as any of such departments of FTSE 100 or NYSE-listed organisations.

With technology exponentially advancing, and with terrorist groups seeming to be so far ahead of government officials in using, unabated, all the technology the internet abounds with, the governments must act – they must engage these groups on what has become an online battlefield. Social media platform owners need to be involved and active participants in stopping terrorist organisations from using and abusing their platforms to post inflammatory rhetoric and encourage their followers to conduct jihad.

If the international organisations and national governments fail to use their own human capital's innovative minds to counter online extremism, they lose out on a real opportunity to change the balance of power against the use of internet for terrorism purposes (Institute for Economics & Peace 2016). Terrorist organisations are fighting on many fronts – for ISIS, the online community was critical to its ability to attract financial support and to recruit additional fighters.

The national and cross-border intelligence agencies should use specific measures to combat the enticement of disenfranchised individuals by extremist groups and the spreading of their propaganda via online platforms. To do this effectively, these agencies must fully understand the current challenges facing predominately the Muslim youth and those particularly vulnerable to calls to participate in violent jihad. Countermeasures should include, among others, an in-depth education about the diverse history and heritage of the Middle East and North Africa (Woolf 2016).

Another opportunity the international community should consider is the encouragement of additional crowdsourcing campaigns similar to the one employed by the Counter Extremism Project, which was mainly put in place in order to disrupt the digital propaganda generated by terrorist organisations (Lynch 2014). By highlighting the extremists' tweets and reporting their hateful messages to Twitter and to law enforcement agencies, the project has identified hundreds of extremists as well as people who have called for violent actions and who have made direct threats against others. The intelligence community needs specialised support and actual seasoned communicators/PR experts to debunk propaganda myths and touch the hearts and minds of those who use public social networks as a place of safety to carry out unsocial acts (Gandelman 2016).

There also needs to be a more concerted support for the establishment of a specialised international online crime unit (not just cybercrime) staffed by the best experts in psychology, anthropology, social media, communications and PR its member countries can bring together – this community will need to have a decentralised hub where specialised personnel can begin to monitor, assess, answer and counteract extremist sentiments online with photos and videos to undercut terrorist organisations and disrupt their messages (Livingston 2014). Such enterprise should be allowed to continually revise its strategies and tactics, to report on its success rate and to have a high degree of flexibility – ISIS had a very strong 'marketing' campaign supporting its 'brand'; the international community does not (Weimann 2016).

A significant number of international governments endeavour to prohibit objectionable material from being seen or spread online – for instance, spreading hate speech. The international community and intelligence agencies need to look for ways to legally prohibit the online spread of terrorist propaganda (Bar-Ilan et al. 2015). In some countries, such as the US, it is unlawful for citizens to knowingly give 'material support or resources' to a designated foreign terrorist organisation. Material support is defined as any property, tangible or intangible, or service, including currency or monetary instruments or financial securities, financial services, lodging, training, expert advice or assistance, safehouses, false documentation or identification, communications equipment, facilities, weapons, lethal substances, explosives, personnel and transportation (Wittes 2017).

Some companies are not deterred from working with terrorist organisations because they either don't fear any sort of sanction or prosecution for doing business with these groups or they don't realise these groups are affiliated with terrorism (Giroux 2014). However, there are existing regulations that each government could use against the terrorist activity in cyberspace. For instance, following the 11 September 2001 terrorist attacks, the US Congress passed the Emergency Economic Powers Act. The act gives the US president the power to declare a national emergency to threats against the homeland, the US economy or foreign interests, and allows the president to exercise his authority in investigating and blocking transactions. There are times when authority needs to trump democratic and liberal rights – used wisely, it can work; abusing it, it can lead to a rise in hate speech and extremist acts.

The US' example above could be replicated by other democratic nations, especially since under this act, the Treasury Department can use its authority to issue 'cease and desist' orders to US internet service providers to prevent them from providing material support to foreign terrorist organisations. Such a move may force these groups to seek out overseas companies to host their websites, but the international community can apply the same set of regulations to their own sovereign/common laws to avoid the misuse of the freedoms allowed by social media and the internet (Phyrillas 2015).

In addition to overtly attempting to change the hearts and minds of would-be jihadists, governments across the world should consider conducting regular covert information operations. These would require governments to research the different ways people are using the internet and social media for negative content and disrupt their use/consumption of the same through hacking techniques (Boulton and Zook 2013:437) – as unethical as this practice may be viewed by some, it could be argued that saving innocent lives should trump any invasion of privacy. However, and this is the main criticism that has been brought to democratic governments' surveillance agencies, such disruptive hacking techniques can be very easily abused by those in power to further their political agendas or interests.

Governments' specialised counterintelligence services could leverage their extensive media, technology and intelligence experience to carefully craft and insert anti-terrorism messages to target audiences around the globe. While this approach has begun to be deployed by both the American and UK governments, not enough is being done by the main European governments. ISIS should be singled out for what it is in a concerted multi-national initiative, making it brutally and blatantly clear that it is a far cry from the puritan values- and beliefs-driven Islamic group that it claims to be (Timreck 2017).

It is through social media that messages of terrorism and populist movements proved successful in the last decade. Governments can and should collaborate with social media platforms owners to find a permanent yet 'living' solution of how to timely address the situation of the social media accounts purporting terrorism (Levine 2011). Government officials should continue to pressure social media providers such as Facebook, WhatsApp, Twitter, VKontakte and others to increase their monitoring and termination of accounts belonging to potential terrorist supporters, although, realistically, it will not be possible to shut down every single account. However, by removing a significant number of such accounts, the access to radicalising narratives for those interested in jihad could be slowed down. To become radicalised, a person follows a cognitive, conscious process of gathering information and talking to like-minded people.

Suspending social media accounts would make finding extremist content materials much more difficult. If such suspensions continue at a regular pace, it will be more difficult for ISIS members and supporters to keep up and regenerate accounts (Aistrope 2016:121), and there are certain actions social media platform providers could take to assist the international security efforts, one of which would be providing the national governments, intelligence agencies, interagency law enforcement, task forces and other selected partners a special expedited-reporting mechanism so that they can swiftly notify Twitter, for instance, of any objectionable content and have the platform take it down (US Navy 2015).

This would allow vetted security and intelligence personnel with direct access to those in charge of monitoring content for Twitter, for instance, so that they could circumvent Twitter's often complicated and cumbersome reporting process. Social media platforms could also streamline, should they choose to, their reporting processes. Today, if someone wants to report a tweet as offensive, it goes into a generic spam category. Twitter has already set up a more streamlined reporting process for women to report harassment. As such, Twitter could set up another reporting category for users to alert the company of tweets associated with terrorist groups or impending terrorist acts (Levine 2011).

As of March 2019, five years after ISIS has pretty much ruled the social media platforms with its technological prowess and messaging might, Twitter still does not have an option of reporting a tweet that clearly reads 'extremist content' or 'inciting to violence'. And it should.

Another solution – yet potentially detrimental to social media platforms' number of followers – may be to compel all their users to verify their accounts. There should be no unverified accounts on social media. Social media platforms' owners should know the identity of everyone using their platforms and, when prompted, they should share this information with the intelligence services and security departments providing, of course, the grounds for such requests are legally justifiable. Those who engage in the spread of hateful, violence-inducing propaganda do not deserve anonymity, and they should be considered as having waivered their right to privacy (Ibrahim 2015).

Non-governmental organisations and social media influencers have an increasingly significant role in the state decision-making process since their voices reach far and wide and are considered to be mostly free of political bias. Public opinion has become much more important in recent years, and the international community (Fishman 2007) could tap into the immense potential of rallying these voices to combat online extremism. A Muslim teenager under the influence of strong jihadi content living in 21st-century Britain or United States is much more likely to be influenced by his/her workmates, college friends or religious congregation than he/she would be by any public appeal made by Prime Minister May or President Trump.

ISIS is not an extremist faction created by the social media platforms or the internet – it was empowered by them. ISIS is the embodiment, first and foremost, of a centuries-old political phenomenon which, likely, will take several more centuries to finally settle. The technological advancements of the 21st century conferred ISIS a voice and a means to reaching, enticing and attracting thousands of sympathisers across the world, both Muslims and non-Muslims, women and men, Arabs and non-Arabs. A propaganda strategy can only be counteracted by deploying the same mechanism that created that strategy to begin with – in ISIS' case, that includes a wealth of psychological value-based triggers underpinned by state-of-the-art visual and audio supports. The international community may not hold the solution to the complex online extremism ISIS developed, but it can ensure that the best-equipped actors and means are deployed to counter it.

ISIS' social media engagement approach and style is, indeed, a 21st-century challenge for the international community. Lessons need to be learned, and appropriate strategies of combating online extremism need to be found sooner rather than later – ISIS may well be just the beginning, and it is up to the international community to make sure that ISIS is also the end.

Extremism, either jihadi or white, as demonstrated throughout this book, is the product of a multitude of socio-economic factors underpinned by psychological triggers. Extremists, to find a comparison to concepts pervasive across the corporate world, can be compared to disgruntled customers or employees. As one would persuade a customer to continue purchasing a product or using a service, or as one would ensure that an employee's complaints are heard and dealt with to the extent possible, the same approach should be employed when dealing with online extremism – ISIS not only just marked the beginning of a new form of extremist jihadi engagement and communication, it also showed that it is possible to use free speech and open platforms of communication to sow hatred, revenge and terror.

In a social media age where the relationships between organisations and their publics are no longer bound by physical barriers or insufficient/improper access to communication channels, Harlow's (1976) analysis of 472 definitions of PR stands more true today than it ever has before:

> Public relations is the distinctive management function which helps establish and maintain mutual lines of communication, understanding, acceptance and cooperation between an organization and its publics; involves the

management of problems or issues; helps management to keep informed on and responsive to public opinion; defines and emphasizes the responsibility of management to serve the public interest; helps management keep abreast of and effectively utilize change, serving as an early warning system to help anticipate trends; and uses research and sound and ethical communication as its principal tools.

BIBLIOGRAPHY

Abbasi, Aamir. 2017. 'Is #Terrorism Strictly a #PR Exercise and What About #Counterterrorism?'. *LinkedIn*, www.linkedin.com/pulse/terrorism-strictly-pr-exercise-what-counterterrorism-abbasi-cipr-?published=t (accessed 8 July 2017).

Abbruzzese, Jason. 2018. 'Facebook Hits 2.27 Billion Monthly Active Users as Earnings Stabilize'. *NBC News*, www.nbcnews.com/tech/tech-news/facebook-hits-2-27-billion-monthly-active-users-earnings-stabilize-n926391 (accessed 25 March 2019).

Accad, Martin. 2015. 'Beating Back ISIS'. *The Institute of Middle East Studies*, https://imes.blog/2015/02/20/beating-back-isis/ (accessed 19 September 2017).

ADL. 2016. 'New ISIS Threat Campaign Capitalizes on Paris Attacks'. *Anti-Defamation League*, www.adl.org/blog/new-isis-threat-campaign-capitalizes-on-paris-attacks (accessed 29 May 2017).

Aistrope, Tim. 2016. 'Social Media and Counterterrorism Strategy'. *Australian Journal of International Affairs*, 70, pp. 121–138.

Al-Barghouti, Tamim. 2008. *The Umma and the Dawla*. London: Pluto Press.

'Al-Qaida and ISIS Use Twitter Differently. Here's How and Why'. *National Journal Daily*, 9 October 2014. (Laura Ryan).

Al-Tamimi, Aymenn Jawad. 2014. 'Iraqis, Saudis Call Shots In Raqqa, ISIL's Syrian "Capital"'. *Aymenn Jawad*, www.aymennjawad.org/14925/iraqis-saudis-call-shots-in-raqqa-isil-syrian (accessed 21 February 2017).

Alcorn, Chauncey L. 2016. 'Here's What Tech ISIS Is Using to Spread Its Message'. *Fortune*, http://fortune.com/2016/07/25/isis-terrorists-tech-android-iphone/ (accessed 25 March 2019).

Altheide, David L. 2016. *The Media Syndrome*. Abingdon: Taylor and Francis.

Anonymous. 2016. 'ISIS Leader Communicates Through Media'. *Investigative Project on Terrorism*, https://www.investigativeproject.org/documents/case.../3028.pdf (accessed 22 June 2019).

Anonymous. 2017. 'EU Leaders Urge Internet Giants to Fight Online Extremism'. *Phys Org*, https://phys.org/news/2017-06-eu-leaders-urge-internet-giants.html (accessed 18 September 2017).

Ashton, Baroness Cathy. 2016. 'MA International Affairs and Diplomacy'. University of Buckingham Evening Seminar.

Atwan, Abdel Bari. 2015. *Islamic State*. London: Saqi Books.

Awbrey, Susan M. 2006. *Integrative Learning and Action*. New York: Peter Lang.

Bar-Ilan, Judit, Timothy D. Bowman, Stefanie Haustein, Staša Milojević and Isabella Peters. 2015. 'Self-Presentation in Academia Today: From Peer-Reviewed Publications to Social Media'. *Proceedings of the Association for Information Science and Technology*, 52.

Barnett, Antony. 2004. 'Islamic Rappers' Message of Terror'. *The Guardian*, www.the-guardian.com/uk/2004/feb/08/arts.politics (accessed 21 September 2017).

Barrett, Richard. 2014. 'Foreign Fighters In Syria'. *The Soufan Group*, http://soufangroup.com/wp-content/uploads/2014/06/TSG-Foreign-Fighters-in-Syria.pdf (accessed 25 April 2017).

Barrett, Richard. 2017. 'Beyond the Caliphate: Foreign Fighters and the Threat of Returnees'. *The Soufan Center*, www.google.co.uk/url?sa=t&rct=j&q=&esrc=s&sou rce=web&cd=9&cad=rja&uact=8&ved=2ahUKEwjbjN_dwfXgAhVZXhUIHXR mAX4QFjAIegQIBBAC&url=https%3A%2F%2Fthesoufancenter.org%2Fwp-conte nt%2Fuploads%2F2017%2F11%2FBeyond-the-Caliphate-Foreign-Fighters-and-the-Threat-of-Returnees-TSC-Report-October-2017-v3.pdf&usg=AOvVaw1-q9N4H-vTCllLZqkyIZyr (accessed 25 March 2019).

Barrow, Victoria. 2015. 'ISIS Recruitment: Social Media, Isolation, and Manipulation'. *Citizens for Global Solutions*, http://globalsolutions.org/blog/2015/12/ISIS-Recruitment-Social-Media-Isolation-and-Manipulation#.WYHUVYTyvIV (accessed 19 September 2017).

Bates, Robin. 2015. 'ISIS Mastermind Like Mystery Cat Macavity'. *Better Living Through Beowulf*, http://betterlivingthroughbeowulf.com/isis-mastermind-like-mystery-cat-macavity/ (accessed 20 September 2017).

BBC Radio 4. 2017. 'The Revolution Will Be Tweeted'. *Friends & Family – A Narrative History of Diplomacy*, www.bbc.co.uk/programmes/b08drjdx (accessed 11 March 2017).

Bedard, Paul. 2017. 'FBI's Comey: 15% of Terrorists Came to US as Refugees, at Least 300'. *Washington Examiner*, www.washingtonexaminer.com/fbis-comey-15-of-terrorists-came-to-us-as-refugees-at-least-300 (accessed 26 March 2019).

Beeman, Hadley. 2017. 'Where Terrorists Go to Chat'. *Medium*, https://medium.com/@ hadleybeeman/where-terrorists-go-to-chat-2943e47cbefc (accessed 2 May 2017).

Benedetto, Francesco and Antonio Tedeschi. 2016. 'Data Sentiment Analysis for Brand Monitoring in Social Media Streams by Cloud Computing'. In *Sentiment Analysis and Ontology Engineering*. Cham: Springer International Publishing.

Benson, Merv. 2015. 'Targeting ISIS Through Social Media'. *Prairie Pundit*, http://prairi-epundit.blogspot.co.uk/2015/06/targeting-isil-through-social-media.html (accessed September 2017).

Berger, J.M. and Jonathon Morgan. 2015. 'The ISIS Twitter Consensus: Defining and Describing the Population of ISIS Supporters on Twitter'. *Analysis Paper*, 20. Washington DC: The Brookings Institution, www.brookings.edu/wp-content/uploads/2016/06/isis_twitter_census_berger_morgan.pdf (accessed 10 October 2017).

Berger, J.M. and Heather Perez. 2016. 'The Islamic State's Diminishing Returns on Twitter: How Suspensions Are Limiting the Social Networks of English-Speaking ISIS Supporters'. *George Washington University, Program on Extremism*, https://cchs.gwu.edu/sites/cchs.gwu.edu/files/. . ./Berger_Occasional%20Paper.pdf (accessed 10 November 2017).

Bishop, Donald M. 2016a. 'Quotable: NATO Centre on Social Media as a Tool of Hybrid Warfare'. *Public Diplomacy Council*, www.publicdiplomacycouncil.org/com mentaries/07-10-16/quotable-nato-centre-social-media-tool-hybrid-warfare (accessed 19 September 2017).

Bishop, Donald M. 2016b. 'Quotable: Richard Stengel on ISIS Messaging and Social Media'. *Public Diplomacy Council*, www.publicdiplomacycouncil.org/commentaries/02-09-16/quotable-richard-stengel-isis-messaging-and-social-media (accessed 10 November 2017).

Blair, Tony. 2011. 'Full Transcript of Tony Blair's Statement'. *The Guardian*, https://www.theguardian.com/world/2001/sep/11/september11.usa23 (accessed 21 June 2019).

Blaker, Lisa. 2015. 'The Islamic State's Use of Online Social Media'. *Military Cyber Affairs*, 1.

Bleiker, Roland and Emma Hutchinson. 2008. 'Fear No More: Emotions and World Politics'. *Review of International Studies*, 34, pp. 115–135.

Bloom, Mia. 2016. 'Constructing Expertise: Terrorist Recruitment and "Talent Spotting" in the PIRA, Al Qaeda, and ISIS'. *Studies in Conflict & Terrorism*, 40.

Bodine-Baron, Elizabeth. 2016. 'Fighting the Islamic State on Social Media'. *Rand*, www.rand.org/blog/2016/10/fighting-the-islamic-state-on-social-media.html (accessed 20 September 2017).

Bodine-Baron, Elizabeth A., Todd Helmus C., Madeline Magnuson and Zev Winkelman. 2016. *Examining ISIS Support and Opposition Networks on Twitter*. Santa Monica: Rand Corporation.

Boffey, Daniel. 2015. 'David Cameron Announces Funding for Anti-Extremism Strategy'. *The Guardian*, www.theguardian.com/politics/2015/oct/18/cameron-funding-anti-extremism-social-media (accessed 10 October 2017).

Boulton, Andrew and Matthew Zook. 2013. 'Landscape, Locative Media, and the Duplicity of Code'. In *Cultural Geography*. Nuala C. Johnson, Richard H. Schein, Jamie Winders (eds.). Oxford: Wiley, pp. 437–451.

Briggs, Rachel and Sebastien Feve. 2013. 'Review of Programs to Counter Narratives of Violent Extremism: What Works and What Are the Implications for Government?'. *Counter Extremism*, www.counterextremism.org/resources/details/id/444/review-of-programs-to-counter-narratives-of-violent-extremism-what-works-and-what-are-the-implications-for-government (accessed 21 September 2017).

British Foreign Policy Group. 2017. 'Digital Disruption, Social Media and UK Foreign Policy Meeting Notes'. *Chatham House*.

Brooking, Emerson and Peter W. Singer. 2016. 'The War on Social Media'. *Popular Science*, 288, pp. 60–65.

Brooten, Lisa. 2011. 'Media, Militarization, and Human Rights: Comparing Media Reform in the Philippines and Burma'. *Communication, Culture & Critique*, 4.

Brown, Daniel. 2018. 'Weapons Sales Are on the Rise – Here Are the Top 10 Countries Exporting Arms Around the World'. *Business Insider*, www.businessinsider.com/top-countries-exporting-weapons-arms-sales-2018-3?r=US&IR=T (accessed 26 March 2019).

Brynjar, Lia. 2015. 'The Islamic State (IS) and Its Mediatized Barbarism'. *The New Middle East Blog*, https://newmeast.wordpress.com/2015/03/14/the-islamic-state-is-and-its-mediatized-barbarism/ (accessed 19 September 2017).

Burke, Jason. 2015. *The New Threat From Islamic Militancy*. London: The Bodley Head, pp. 4–5, 88, 102, 103, 175, 180, 205, 211, 213, 242.

Callimachi, Rukmini. 2015. 'Clues on Twitter Show Ties Between Texas Gunman and ISIS Network'. *The New York Times*, www.nytimes.com/2015/05/12/us/twitter-clues-show-ties-between-isis-and-garland-texas-gunman.html (accessed 26 March 2019).

Callimachi, Rukmini. 2018. 'ISIS Leader Baghdadi Resurfaces in Recording'. *The New York Times*, www.nytimes.com/2018/08/22/world/middleeast/isis-leader-baghdadi-recording.html (accessed 26 March 2019).

Campbell, David. 2003. 'Cultural Governance and Pictorial Resistance: Reflections on the Imagining of War'. *Review of International Studies*, 29, pp. 57–73.

Carman, Ashley. 2015. 'Filtered Extremism: How ISIS Supporters Use Instagram'. *The Verge*, www.theverge.com/2015/12/9/9879308/isis-instagram-islamic-state-social-media (accessed 21 September 2017).

Castells, Manuel. 2013. *Communication Power*. Oxford: Oxford University Press.

Chavez, Nicole, Holly Yan, Eric Levenson and Steve Almasy. 2017. 'New York Attack: Suspect Charged with Terrorism Offenses'. *CNN*, http://edition.cnn.com/2017/11/01/us/new-york-attack/index.html (accessed 1 November 2017).

Cheshire, Tom. 2017. 'How IS Has Changed Its Online Message'. *Sky News*, http://news.sky.com/story/how-islamic-state-has-changed-its-online-message-10811895 (accessed 24 May 2017).

Clarke-Billings, Lucy. 2015. 'ISIS Targets Australian Teenagers to Join 'Death Cult' Amid Fears They Will Be Used as Cannon Fodder'. *The Independent*, www.independent.co.uk/news/world/middle-east/isis-targets-australian-teenagers-to-join-death-cult-amid-fearsthey-will-be-used-as-cannon-fodder-10095342.html (accessed 21 April 2017).

Clint, Edward. 2015. 'Twitterdom and Social Media Duped by Fake Putin Quote – Incredulous'. *Skeptic Ink*, www.skepticink.com/incredulous/2015/11/18/fox-news-twitterdom-and-social-media-duped-by-fake-putin-quote/ (accessed 26 March 2019).

Cockburn, Patrick. 2016. *The Age of Jihad: Islamic State and the Great War for the Middle East*. London: Verso.

Cohen, Jared. 2016. 'Islamic State of Iraq and Syria (ISIS)'. *Chatham House*, www.chathamhouse.org/file/jared-cohen-director-google-ideas-advisor-executive-chairman-alphabet-inc (accessed 6 June 2017).

Cohen, Jean L. 1985. 'Strategy or Identity: New Theoretical Paradigms and Contemporary Social Movements'. *Social Research*, 53, pp. 663–716.

Committee on Homeland Security and Governmental Affairs. 2016. 'ISIS Online: Countering Terrorist Radicalization and Recruitment on the Internet and Social Media'. *United States Government Publishing Office*, https://archive.org/details/gov.gpo.fdsys.CHRG-114shrg22476 (accessed 11 March 2017).

Condon, Camie and Jeff Weyers. 2015. 'Ibrabo'. *Ibrabo*, https://ibrabo.wordpress.com/ (accessed 6 June 2017).

Coolsaet, Rik. 2015. 'Egmont Paper 75: What Drives Europeans to Syria, and to IS? Insights from the Belgian Case'. *Egmont Institute*, www.egmontinstitute.be/content/uploads/2015/03/75.pdf?type=pdf (accessed 21 September 2017).

Cooper, Helene. 2016. 'Boko Haram and ISIS Are Collaborating More, U.S. Military Says'. *The New York Times*, https://www.nytimes.com/2016/04/21/world/africa/boko-haram-and-isis-are-collaborating-more-us-military-says.html (accessed 18 June 2019).

Cooper, Paige. 2019. '28 Twitter Statistics All Marketers Need to Know in 2019'. *Hootsuite*, https://blog.hootsuite.com/twitter-statistics/ (accessed 25 March 2019).

Cooper, Robert. 2017. 'The Revolution Will Be Tweeted'. *Friends & Family – A Narrative History of Diplomacy*, www.bbc.co.uk/programmes/b08drjdx (accessed 18 September 2017).

'Counter Extremism Project CEO Mark Wallace to Testify Before House Committee on Foreign Affairs'. 2015. *Counter Extremism Project*, www.counterextremism.com/press/counter-extremism-project-ceo-mark-wallace-testify-house-committee-foreign-affairs (accessed 21 September 2017).

Cribb, Ceighley. 2016. 'ISIS Recruitment'. *Peacefare*, www.peacefare.net/2016/02/29/isis-recruitment/ (accessed 19 September 2017).

Curtis, Mark. 2003. *Web of Deceit: Britain's Real Foreign Policy: Britain's Real Role in the World*. London: Vintage.

Davis, Eric. 2014. 'ISIS's Strategic Threat: Ideology, Recruitment, Political Economy'. *The New Middle East*, http://new-middle-east.blogspot.co.uk/2014/08/isiss-strategic-threat-ideology.html (accessed 19 September 2017).

'Digital 2019'. 2019. *We Are Social*, https://wearesocial.com/blog/2019/01/digital-2019-global-internet-use-accelerates (accessed 25 February 2019).

diMaggio, Paul, Eszter Hargitai, Russell W. Neuman and John P. Robinson, 2001. 'Social Implications of the Internet'. *Annual Review of Sociology*, 27, pp. 307–336.

Disinformation and 'Fake News': Final Report. Eighth Report of Session 2017–19. 2019. House of Commons – Digital, Culture, Media and Sport Committee, https://publications.parliament.uk/pa/cm201719/cmselect/cmcumeds/1791/1791.pdf (accessed 25 March 2019).

Dowd, Maureen. 2014. 'Back to Iraq'. *The New York Times*, https://www.nytimes.com/2014/08/10/opinion/sunday/maureen-dowd-back-to-iraq.html (accessed 22 June 2014).

Eckardt, Andy. 2015. 'Denis Cuspert, AKA "Deso Dogg," Named By U.S. as ISIS Terrorist'. *NBC News*, www.nbcnews.com/storyline/isis-terror/denis-cuspert-aka-deso-dogg-named-u-s-isisterrorist-n303456 (accessed 25 April 2017).

Elgot, Jessica. 2015. 'Xi Jinping UK Visit Roundup: Red Flags, Red Carpets and Greene King'. *The Guardian*, www.theguardian.com/world/2015/oct/23/chinese-president-xi-jinping-uk-visit-roundup (accessed September 2017).

Elson, Sara Beth. 2012. *Using Social Media to Gauge Iranian Public Opinion and Mood After the 2009 Election*. Santa Monica: RAND.

Engel, Pamela. 2015. 'This Scottish Teenager Went From Reading Harry Potter to Recruiting for ISIS In Syria'. *Business Insider*, http://uk.businessinsider.com/how-aqsa-mahmood-ended-up-recruiting-for-isis-in-syria-2015-2 (accessed 12 April 2017).

Erelle, Anna. 2015. *In the Skin of a Jihadist: A Young Journalist Enters the ISIS Recruitment Network in a Daring and Revelatory Investigation*. London: Harper Paperbacks.

'EU Referendum: The Result in Maps and Charts'. 2016. *BBC News*, www.bbc.com/news/uk-politics-36616028 (accessed 25 March 2019).

'Europol's Internet Referral Unit to Combat Terrorist and Violent Extremist Propaganda'. 2015. *Europol*, www.europol.europa.eu/newsroom/news/europol%E2%80%99s-internet-referral-unit-to-combat-terrorist-and-violent-extremist-propaganda (accessed 23 October 2017).

'Extremism, Terrorism and Strategic Communication'. 2019. *International Centre for the Study of Radicalisation*, https://icsr.info/our-work/extremism-terrorism-and-strategic-communication/ (accessed 26 March 2019).

Faris, David M. and Rahimi Babak. 2015. *Social Media in Iran: Politics and Society After 2009*. New York: University Press, p. 60.

Farwell, James P. 2014. 'The Media Strategy of ISIS'. *Survival*, 56.

Feldman, David. 2016. 'Service of Process by Social Media? Yep'. *David Feldman Blog*, www.davidfeldmanblog.com/service-of-process-by-social-media-yep/ (accessed 20 September 2017).

Fernandez, Alberto M. 2015. 'Four Ways to Counter ISIS Propaganda More Effectively'. *The Brookings Institution*, www.brookings.edu/blog/markaz/2015/11/16/four-ways-to-counter-isis-propaganda-more-effectively/ (accessed 30 May 2017).

Field, Matthew. 2018. 'Apple Removes Encrypted Messaging App Telegram From App Store'. *The Telegraph*, www.telegraph.co.uk/technology/2018/02/01/apple-removes-encrypted-messaging-app-telegram-app-store/ (accessed 26 March 2019).

Fishman, Brian. 2007. 'Fourth Generation Governance – Sheikh Tamimi Defends the Islamic State of Iraq'. *Defense Technical Information Centre.*

Fleming, Sean. 2019. 'This NATO Experiment Used Fake Facebook Accounts to Trick Soldiers into Sharing Sensitive Information'. *World Economic Forum*, www.weforum. org/agenda/2019/03/nato-experiment-faked-facebook-for-soldier-data (accessed 25 March 2019).

Fletcher, Tom. 2016. *Naked Diplomacy: Power and Statecraft in the Digital Age.* London: William Collins.

'Foreign Fighters – An Updated Assessment of the Flow of Foreign Fighters into Syria and Iraq'. 2015. *The Soufan Group*, http://soufangroup.com/wp-content/uploads/2015/12/TSG_ForeignFightersUpdate3.pdf (accessed 21 September 2017).

Friis, Simone M. 2015. '"Beyond Anything We Have Ever Seen": Beheading Videos and the Visibility of Violence in the War Against ISIS'. *International Affairs*, 91, pp. 725–746.

Fuchs, Christian. 2014. 'Social Media and the Islamic State's Killing of James Foley: Why It Is Time the West Shifts Public Attention Towards the Kurdish Internet-Sphere'. *Fuchs*, http://fuchs.uti.at/1200/ (accessed 21 July 2017).

Fulton, Barry. 2002. *Net Diplomacy: 2015 and Beyond.* Washington, DC: United States Institute of Peace.

Gallarati, Livia. 2016. 'Fighting ISIS on Social Media: Ideas for an Individualized Approach'. *Take Five | Blog of the Institute for Public Diplomacy and Global Communication*, https://takefiveblog.org/2016/04/28/fighting-isis-on-social-media-ideas-for-an-individualized-approach/ (accessed 18 September 2017).

Gambhir, Harleen. 2016. *The Virtual Caliphate: ISIS's Information Warfare.* Washington: Institute for the Study of War.

Gandelman, Joe. 2016. 'World, Media, Social Media Reaction to Orlando Gay Nightclub Shootings (Updated)'. *The Moderate Voice*, http://themoderatevoice.com/world-media-twitter-reaction-to-orlando-gay-nightclub-shootings/ (accessed 20 September 2017).

Garcia, Regina A. and Al-Khalifa, Hend S. 2013. 'The State of Social Media in Saudi Arabia's Higher Education'. *International Journal of Technology and Educational Marketing*, 3, pp. 65–76.

Gartenstein-Ross, Daveed. 2015. 'Ansar Bayt Al-Maqdis's Oath of Allegiance to the Islamic State'. *Wikistrat*, www.google.co.uk/url?sa=t&rct=j&q=&esrc=s&source=web&cd=1&cad=rja&uact=8&ved=2ahUKEwj41vWk3pXhAhVZXhUIHcjZAX0QFjAAegQIBhAC&url=http%3A%2F%2Fwww.fdd.org%2Fcontent%2Fuploads%2Fdocuments%2FAnsar-Bayt-Al-Maqdis-Oath-of-Allegiance-to-the-Islamic-State-Wikistrat-Report.pdf&usg=AOvVaw3Fk5Xm9g4fNo-Tr9sCNFs8 (accessed 22 March 2019).

Gatehouse, Gabriel. 2016. 'Top IS commanders "taking refuge" in Libya'. *BBC Newsnight*, https://www.bbc.co.uk/news/world-africa-35486158 (accessed 18 June 2019).

Gayle, Damien. 2019. 'UK Military Turns to Universities to Research Psychological Warfare'. *The Guardian*, www.theguardian.com/uk-news/2019/mar/13/uk-military-mod-universities-research-psychological-warfare-documents (accessed 26 March 2019).

Gerges, Fawaz A. 2016. *ISIS: A History.* New York: Princeton University Press.

Gibson, Steven and Agnes Lucy Lando. 2016. *Impact of Communication and the Media on Ethnic Conflict.* Hershey, PA: IGI Global.

Gilbert, David. 2015. 'ISIS Moves to the Dark Web to Spread Its Message and Avoid Detection'. *International Business Times*, www.ibtimes.com/isis-moves-dark-web-spread-its-message-avoid-detection-2191593 (accessed 21 September 2017).

'Girl Talk: Calling Western Women to Syria'. 2014. *Insite Blog*, http://news.siteintel group.com/blog/index.php/about-us/21-jihad/4406-girl-talk-calling-western-women-to-syria (accessed 1 May 2017).

Giroux, Henry A. 2014. 'ISIS and the Spectacle of Terrorism: Resisting Mainstream Workstations of Fear'. *Truth Out*, www.truth-out.org/news/item/26519-isis-and-the-spectacle-of-terrorism-resisting-mainstream-workstations-of-fear (accessed 19 September 2017).

Golan, Guy J., Yang Sung-Un and Dennis F. Kinsey. 2014. *International Public Relations and Public Diplomacy: Communication and Engagement*. New York: Peter Lang Publishing Inc.

Goldman, Adam and Eric Schmitt. 2016. 'One by One, ISIS Social Media Experts Are Killed as Result of F.B.I. Program'. *New York Times*, www.nytimes.com/2016/11/24/world/middleeast/isis-recruiters-social-media.html?mcubz=1 (accessed 18 September 2017).

Javid, Sajid and Ben Wallace. 2019. 'Counter-Terrorism and Border Security Bill Given Royal Assent'. *GOV.UK*, https://www.gov.uk/government/news/counter-terrorism-and-border-security-bill-given-royal-assent (accessed 19 June 2019).

Grierson, Jamie. 2019. 'Shamima Begum's Mother Asks Home Office to Show Mercy'. *The Guardian*, www.theguardian.com/uk-news/2019/mar/11/shamima-begum-mother-asks-home-office-to-show-mercy (accessed 26 March 2019).

Griffing, Alexander. 2018. 'How Assad Helped Create ISIS to Win in Syria and Got Away With the Crime of the Century'. *Haaretz*, www.haaretz.com/middle-east-news/syria/MAGAZINE-iran-russia-and-isis-how-assad-won-in-syria-1.6462751 (accessed 26 March 2019).

Hai-Jew, Shalin. 2017. 'Social Media Listening and Monitoring for Media Application – Chapter: Real-Time Sentiment Analysis of Microblog Messages with the Maltego "Tweet Analyzer" Machine'. *IGI Global*, www.igi-global.com/chapter/real-time-sentiment-analysis-of-microblog-messages-with-the-maltego-tweet-analyzer-machine/166454 (accessed 4 July 2017).

Hall, Benjamin. 2015. *Inside ISIS: The Brutal Rise of a Terrorist Army*. New York: Centre Street.

Haq, Husna. 2014. 'ISIS Excels at Recruiting American Teens: Here Are Four Reasons Why'. *The Christian Science Monitor*, www.csmonitor.com/USA/USA-Update/2014/1022/ISIS-excels-at-recruiting-American-teens-Here-are-four-reasons-why-video (accessed 25 April 2017).

Harlow, Rex F. 1976. 'Building a public relations definition'. *Public Relations Review*, 2(4), pp. 34–42.

Harris, David. 2014. 'The Islamic State's (ISIS, ISIL) Magazine'. *Clarion Project*, https://clarionproject.org/islamic-state-isis-isil-propaganda-magazine-dabiq-50/ (accessed 21 September 2017).

Harwell, Drew. 2019. *Twitter*, https://twitter.com/drewharwell/status/1106403560969904128 (accessed 26 March 2019).

Hassan, Hassan. 2016. 'The Sectarianism of the Islamic State: Ideological Roots and Political Context'. *Carnegie Endowment for International Peace*, https://carnegieendowment.org/2016/06/13/sectarianism-of-islamic-state-ideological-roots-and-political-context-pub-63746 (accessed 26 March 2019).

Hénin, Nicolas. 2015. 'I Was Held Hostage By ISIS. They Fear Our Unity More Than Our Airstrikes'. *The Guardian*, www.theguardian.com/commentisfree/2015/nov/16/isis-bombs-hostage-syria-islamic-state-paris-attacks (accessed 1 June 2017).

Herridge, Catherine. 2015. 'ISIS Leader Warns Unauthorized Tweets Don't Speak for Caliphate'. *Fox News*, www.foxnews.com/world/2015/02/02/listen-to-me-isis-leader-warns-unauthorized-tweets-dont-speak-for-caliphate.html (accessed 21 September 2017).

Hoffman, Michael. 2015. 'US Air Force Targets and Destroys ISIS HQ Building Using Social Media'. *Defense Tech*, www.defensetech.org/2015/06/03/us-air-force-targets-and-destroys-isis-hq-building-using-social-media/ (accessed 19 September 2017).

Hofstede, Geert, Gert Jan Hofstede and Michael Minkov. 2010. *Cultures and Organizations: Software of the Mind* (revised and expanded 3rd ed.). New York: McGraw-Hill.

Holl-Lute, Jane. 2017. 'The Revolution Will Be Tweeted'. *BBC Radio 4 Friends & Family – A Narrative History of Diplomacy*, www.bbc.co.uk/programmes/b08drjdx (accessed 18 September 2017).

Homeland Security. 2016. 'ISIS Online: Countering Terrorist Radicalization and Recruitment on the Internet and Social Media: Hearing Before the Permanent Subcommittee on Investigations of the Committee on Homeland Security and Governmental Affairs, United States Senate, One Hundred Fourteenth Congress, Second Session, July 6, 2016'. *Homeland Security Digital Library*, www.hsdl.org/?abstract&did=798423 (accessed 19 September 2017).

Home Office. 2019. 'Counter-Terrorism and Border Security Bill given Royal Assent'. *Gov.uk*, www.gov.uk/government/news/counter-terrorism-and-border-security-bill-given-royal-assent (accessed 26 March 2019).

Hondula, David M. and Rashmi Krishnamurthy. 'Emergency Management in the Era of Social Media'. *Public Administration Review*, 74.

Hookham, Mark. 2018. 'Army Targets Muslims and Women in New Recruitment Ads'. *The Times*, www.thetimes.co.uk/article/army-targets-muslims-and-women-in-new-recruitment-ads-q0qh995dv (accessed 26 March 2019).

Howard-Jones, Paul. 2016. 'The Impact of Digital Technologies on Human Wellbeing: Evidence From the Sciences of Mind and Brain'. *Nominet Trust*, www.google.co.uk/url?sa=t&rct=j&q=&esrc=s&source=web&cd=1&cad=rja&uact=8&ved=2ahUKEwiwh7X2qp_hAhUSM-wKHfhbBzUQFjAAegQIAxAC&url=https%3A%2F%2Fwww.thechildrensmediafoundation.org%2Fwp-content%2Fuploads%2F2014%2F02%2FHoward-Jones-2011-impact-digital-technologies-on-wellbeing-copy.pdf&usg=AOvVaw0WeGyfgcw5Eg6qFr32gbgV (accessed 26 March 2019).

Hudson, Rex A. 1999. 'The Sociology and Psychology of Terrorism: Who Becomes a Terrorist and Why?'. In *Library of Congress Federal Research Division*. Marilyn Majeska (ed.). Washington, DC: Library of Congress, p. 59.

Hurn, Brian J. and Barry Tomalin. 2013. *Cross-Cultural Communication: Theory and Practice*. Hampshire: Palgrave Macmillan, p. 16.

Ibish, Hussein. 2015. 'The ISIS Theatre of Cruelty'. *New York Times*, www.nytimes.com/2015/02/19/opinion/the-isis-theater-of-cruelty.html?_r=1 (accessed 29 May 2017).

Ibrahim, Ayman S. 2015. '4 Ways ISIS Grounds Its Actions in Religion, and Why It Should Matter (COMMENTARY)'. *Washington Post*, https://www.washingtonpost.com/national/religion/4-ways-isis-grounds-its-actions-in-religion-and-why-it-should-matter-commentary/2015/11/16/d7e31278-8ca0-11e5-934c-a369c80822c2_story.html?noredirect=on&utm_term=.17283a41488a (accessed 18 June 2019).

Institute for Economics & Peace. 2016. *Global Terrorism Index 2016 – Measuring and Understanding the Impact of Terrorism*, economicsandpeace.org/wp-content/.../2016/11/Global-Terrorism-Index-2016.2.pdf (accessed 21 June 2019).

Iosifidis, Petros and Mark Wheeler. 2016. 'The Social Media and the Middle East'. In *Public Spheres and Mediated Social Networks in the Western Context and Beyond*. London: Palgrave Macmillan.

'ISIS on the Recruitment Trail'. 2015. *USA Today*, 144, p. 22.

'Islamic Extremism: Common Concern for Muslim and Western Publics'. 2005. *Pew Research Center*, www.pewglobal.org/2005/07/14/islamic-extremism-common-con cern-for-muslim-and-western-publics/ (accessed 25 March 2019).

'The Islamic State's Leadership Style'. 2019. *Orgtheory.Net*, https://orgtheory.wordpress. com/2014/08/27/the-islamic-states-leadership-style/ (accessed 24 March 2019).

'Islamic State: The Same Script, the Same Horror as Militants Test the West's Resolve: ISIS Video Restating Warning to Britain and US to Stay Away May Be Designed to Provoke Action'. 2014. *The Guardian*, September 15, p. 2. (Martin Chulov).

Jackson, David S. 2015. 'Anti-Social Media: When a Nuisance Turns into a Threat'. *The Public Diplomacy Council*, https://uscpublicdiplomacy.org/blog/anti-social-media-when-nuisance-becomes-threat (accessed 18 September 2017).

Jenkins, John. 2016. 'MA International Affairs and Diplomacy'. University of Buckingham Evening Seminar.

Johnson, N. F., M. Zheng, Y. Vorobyeva, A. Gabriel, H. Qi, N. Velasquez and others. 2016. 'New Online Ecology of Adversarial Aggregates: ISIS and Beyond'. *Science*, p. 352.

Jolls, Heather, Anita Alaverdian, Lindsay Adams and Roselle Silva. 2016. 'The View of Muslims and Arabs in America Before and After September 11th'. *The Brookings Institution*, www.csun.edu/~sm60012/GRCS-Files/Muslims-post-9-11.htm (accessed 18 September 2017).

Jones, Christopher. 2015. 'What Is ISIS' Media Strategy?'. *Gates of Nineveh: An Experiment in Blogging Assyriology*, https://gatesofnineveh.wordpress.com/2015/04/22/what-is-isis-media-strategy/ (accessed 19 September 2017).

Just Security. 2015. *The Investigation Into the Islamic State and Social Media*. The Reiss Center on Law and Security at New York University School of Law.

Kamal, Sara and Shu-Chuan Chu. 2012. 'Cultural Differences in Social Media Usage and Beliefs and Attitudes Towards Advertising on Social Media: Findings From Dubai, United Arab Emirates'. *IGI Global*, www.igi-global.com/chapter/cultural-differences-social-media-usage/55565 (accessed 10 April 2017).

Kappas, Arvid. 2017. 'In the Face of Terror: The Need for More Concerted Applied Emotion Research'. *Emotional Researcher*, http://emotionresearcher.com/isre-matters-emotional-intelligence-issue/ (accessed 29 May 2017).

Karaim, Reed. 2016. 'Defeating the Islamic State: Should the U.S. Deploy Ground Troops to Fight ISIS?'. *CQ Researcher*, http://library.cqpress.com/cqresearcher/docu ment.php?id=cqresrre2016040100 (accessed 18 September 2017).

Karam, Joseph. 2016. 'Twitter, ISIS and Social Media Whack-A-Mole'. *Foreign Policy Blogs*, https://foreignpolicyblogs.com/2016/02/09/twitter-isis-social-media-whack-mole/ (accessed 18 September 2017).

Kates, Steve. 2016. 'The Lone Wolf Social Media Group'. *Catallaxy Files*, http://catall axyfiles.com/2016/12/23/the-lone-wolf-social-media-group/ (accessed 18 September 2017).

Kemp, Simon. 'Digital In 2016'. *We Are Social UK*, https://wearesocial.com/uk/special-reports/digital-in-2016 (accessed 21 September 2017).

Kendall, Bridget. 2016. 'MA International Affairs and Diplomacy'. University of Buckingham Evening Seminar.

Khader, Majeed, Neo Loo Seng, Gabriel Ong and Eunice Tan Mingyi. 2016. *Combating Violent Extremism and Radicalization in the Digital Era*. Hershey, PA: IGI Global.

Khomami, Nadia. 2017. 'UK Government Hires M&C Saatchi to Fight Far-Right Threat'. *The Guardian*, www.theguardian.com/world/2017/feb/06/uks-government-hires-advertising-giant-as-it-fights-far-right-threat (accessed 10 October 2017).

Kim, Jim Yong, Paul Romer, Laura Tuck and Tariq Khokhar. 2015. 'Social Media in the Era of ISIS'. *World Bank Blogs*, https://blogs.worldbank.org/publicsphere/social-media-era-isis (accessed 18 September 2017).

King, Garry, Jennifer Pan and Margaret E. Roberts. 2017. 'How the Chinese Government Fabricates Social Media Posts for Strategic Distraction, not Engaged Argument'. *American Political Science Review*, 111(3), pp. 484–501.

Kirkpatrick, David. 2014. '31 Egyptian Soldiers Are Killed as Militants Attack in Sinai'. *New York Times*, www.nytimes.com/2014/10/25/world/middleeast/militants-kill-at-least-26-egyptian-soldiers-in-sinai-peninsula-attack.html (accessed 21 September 2017).

Klausen, Jytte. 2014. 'Tweeting the Jihad: Social Media Networks of Western Foreign Fighters in Syria and Iraq. *Studies in Conflict & Terrorism*, 38, pp. 1–22.

Klein, Adam. 2017. *Fanaticism, Racism, and Rage Online: Corrupting the Digital Sphere*. London: Palgrave Macmillan.

Koetse, Manya. 2015. 'An Introduction to Sina Weibo: Background and Status Quo'. What's on Weibo, www.whatsonweibo.com/sinaweibo/ (accessed 25 March 2019).

Kosoff, Maya. 2016. 'ISIS Has Directly Threatened Mark Zuckerberg and Jack Dorsey'. *Vanity Fair*, https://www.vanityfair.com/news/2016/02/isis-threatens-mark-zuckerberg-and-jack-dorsey (accessed 18 June 2019).

Kozlowska, Hanna. 2014. 'Should We Be Seeing Gruesome Acts? And If So, Where?'. *New York Times*, https://op-talk.blogs.nytimes.com/2014/08/25/should-we-be-seeing-gruesome-acts-and-if-so-where/ (accessed 21 September 2017).

Krane, Fauntin. 2016. *Two Sociological Outlooks on Social Media and ISIS*. Philadelphia: Lighthouse Publishing.

Krauthammer, Charles. 'Our Real Syria Strategy – Containment-Plus'. *Washington Post*, www.washingtonpost.com/opinions/charles-krauthammer-our-real-syria-strategy – containment-plus/2014/09/25/dd8828b2–44e9–11e4–9a15–137aa0153527_story.html?utm_term=.dac46e0acb83 (accessed 21 September 2017).

Krona, Michael. 2014. 'The Geopolitics of ISIS and their Social Media Strategies'. *Michael Krona*, http://michaelkrona.com/the-geopolitics-of-isis-and-their-social-media-strategies/ (accessed 14 January 2018).

Lawfare. 2016. 'Disrupting ISIS Recruitment Online'. *The Lawfare Podcast*, www.lawfareblog.com/lawfare-podcast-disrupting-isis-recruitment-online (accessed 19 September 2017).

Le Bon, Gustave. 2014. *The Crowd: A Study of the Popular Mind* (4th ed.). London: CreateSpace Independent Publishing Platform.

Legget, Jeremy. 2017. 'The Revolution Will Be Tweeted'. *Friends & Family – A Narrative History of Diplomacy*, www.bbc.co.uk/programmes/b08drjdx (accessed 11 March 2017).

Leiner, Barry M., Vinton G. Cerf, David. D. Clark, Robert E. Kahn, Leonard Kleinrock, Daniel C. Lynch and others. 2016. 'Brief History of the Internet'. *Internet Society*, www.internetsociety.org/internet/what-internet/history-internet/brief-history-internet (accessed 21 September 2017).

Lesaca, Javier. 2015. 'Fight Against ISIS Reveals Power of Social Media'. *Brookings*, www.brookings.edu/blog/techtank/2015/11/19/fight-against-isis-reveals-power-of-social-media/ (accessed 25 March 2019).

Levine, Deb. 2011. 'Using Technology, New Media, In the International Terrorist Scene'. *Sexuality Research and Social Policy*, 8.

Lieber, Paul S. and Peter J. Reiley. 2016. 'Countering ISIS's Social Media Influence'. *Special Operations Journal*, 2(1), pp. 47–57.

Lister, Charles R. 2015. *The Islamic State: A Brief Introduction*. Washington, DC: Brookings Institution Press.

Littlefield, Ryan. 2017. 'Cyber Terrorism: Understanding and Preventing Acts of Terror Within Our Cyber Space'. *Littlefield*, https://littlefield.co/cyber-terrorism-understanding-and-preventing-acts-of-terror-within-our-cyber-space-26ae6d53cfbb (accessed 23 October 2017).

Livingston, King. 2014. 'Social Media as the Guerilla Warzone of the Internet'. *Reportr. Net: Alfred Hermida on Media, Technology and Society*.

Lord William Wallace of Saltaire. 2016. 'MA International Affairs and Diplomacy'. University of Buckingham Evening Seminar.

Louw, P. E. 2003. 'The War Against Terrorism: A Public Relations Challenge For the Pentagon'. *International Communication Gazette*, 65, pp. 211–230.

Lynch, John M. 2014. 'Some Comments on Social Media Trends in Medical History'. *Medical History*, 59.

Mabon, Simon and Stephen Royle. 2017. *The Origins of ISIS: The Collapse of Nations and Revolution in the Middle East*. London: I.B. Tauris.

MacDonald, Stuart. 2017. 'Radicalisers as Regulators: An Examination of Dabiq Magazine'. *College of Law & Criminology, Swansea University*.

Mackey, Robert. 2014. 'Iraq Reportedly Blocks Social Networks'. *The New York Times*, www.nytimes.com/2014/06/14/world/middleeast/iraq-reportedly-blocks-social-networks.html (accessed 26 March 2019).

Mahood, Samantha and Halim Rane. 2016. 'Islamist Narratives in ISIS Recruitment Propaganda'. *The Journal of International Communication*, 23(1), pp. 15–35.

Manero, María Luisa Azpíroz. 2015. *Public Diplomacy: European and Latin American Perspectives*. Brussels: Presses Interuniversitaires Europeennes.

Maney, Kevin. 2014. 'An Open Internet Doesn't Equal Freedom'. *Newsweek*, www.newsweek.com/2014/11/28/open-internet-doesnt-equal-freedom-284651.html (accessed 21 September 2017).

Manor, Ilan. 2015. 'The ISIS Social Media Myth'. *Exploring Digital Diplomacy*, https://digdipblog.com/2015/05/17/the-isis-social-media-myth/ (accessed 19 September 2017).

Mansdorf, Irwin J. and Jacob Weinberg. 2003. 'Stress Reactions in Israel in the Face of Terrorism: Two Community Samples'. *Traumatology*, 9(3), pp. 155–168.

Martin, Vanessa. 2000. *Creating an Islamic State*. London: I.B. Tauris.

Marx, Karl and Friedrich Engles. 2015. *The Communist Manifesto*. London: Penguin Classics.

Mastrocinque, Attilio, Giulia Sfameni Gasparro and Concetta Giuffré Scibona. 2012. *Demeter, ISIS, Vesta, and Cybele: Studies in Greek and Roman Religion in Honour of Giulia Sfameni Gasparro*. Stuttgart: Steiner.

McCabe, Thomas R. 2016. 'A Strategy for the ISIS Foreign Fighter Threat'. *Orbis*, 60, pp. 140–153.

McCauley, Robert N. and Thomas E. Lawson. 2002. *Bringing Ritual to Mind: Psychological Foundations of Cultural Forms*. New York: Cambridge University Press.

McKernan, Bethan. 2016. 'ISIS "Destroys Thousands of Years of Culture Almost Overnight" as It Flees Iraqi Army Near Mosul'. *Independent*, www.independent.co.uk/news/world/middle-east/isis-mosul-iraq-army-terrorists-destroy-demolish-nimrud-temples-artefacts-a7418136.html (accessed 26 March 2019).

McLuhan, Marshall. 2009. 'The World Is a Global Village'. *CBC TV*, www.youtube.com/watch?v=HeDnPP6ntic (accessed 21 September 2017).

Meger, Sara. 2014. 'The Political Economy of "Barbarity" and Sexual Violence by Islamic State (ISIS)'. *The Gender and War Project*, p. 234.

Melissen, Jan. 2016. 'Diplomacy in the Digital Age: More Than Twiplomacy'. *Clingendael*, www.clingendael.nl/publication/diplomacy-digital-age-1 (accessed 14 December 2018).

Melki, Jad and May Jabado. 2016. 'Mediated Public Diplomacy of the Islamic State in Iraq and Syria: The Synergistic Use of Terrorism, Social Media and Branding'. *Media and Communication*, 4(2).

Merari, Ariel. 2010. *Driven to Death: Psychological and Social Aspects of Suicide Terrorism.* New York: Oxford University Press.

Miladi, Nouriddine. 2016. 'Power and Citizenship in the Social Media Networks: British Muslims, Crime Prevention and Social Engagement'. In *Religion, Faith and Crime.* London: Palgrave MacMillan, pp. 285–306.

Moisi, Dominique. 2016. 'London Versus ISIS'. *ASPI the Strategist*, www.aspistrategist. org.au/london-versus-isis/ (accessed 18 September 2017).

Molaei, Hamideh. 2014. 'Social Media Usage, Social Relations, and a Sense of Community in Indonesia'. *International Journal of Interactive Communication Systems and Technologies*, 4, pp. 50–63.

Moore, Johnny. 2015. 'ISIS on the Recruitment Trail'. *USA Today*, 144(2842), p. 22.

Morozov, Evgeny. 2012a. *The Net Delusion: How Not to Liberate the World.* London: Penguin.

Morozov, Evgeny. 2012b. *The Net Delusion: The Dark Side of Internet Freedom* (reprint ed.). New York: Public Affairs.

Mueller, John. 2016. 'Assessing ISIS'. *Cato Institute*, www.cato.org/blog/assessing-isis (accessed 26 March 2019).

Mullen, Jethro. 2015. 'What Is ISIS' Appeal for Young People?'. *CNN*, www.cnn. com/2015/02/25/middleeast/isis-kids-propaganda/ (accessed 25 April 2017).

Naff, Thomas and Marvin E. Wolfgang. 2015. 'Changing Patterns of Power in the Middle East'. *Annals of the American Academy of Political and Social Science*, 482, pp. 9–175.

Nance, Malcolm. 2016. *Defeating ISIS: Who They Are, How They Fight, What They Believe.* New York: Skyhorse Publishing.

National Cyber Security Centre. 2016. *Cyber Security Information Sharing Partnership (CiSP)*, www.ncsc.gov.uk/cisp (accessed 23 October 2017).

'Net Neutrality'. 2016. *White House*, www.whitehouse.gov/net-neutrality (accessed 9 June 2017).

Neumann, Peter R. 2016. *Radicalized: New Jihadists and the Threat to the West.* London: I.B.Tauris.

'New Video Message From the Islamic State: "Flames of War II"'. *Jihadology*, https:// jihadology.net/2017/11/29/new-video-message-from-the-islamic-state-flames-of-war-ii/ (accessed 26 March 2019).

Nichols, Laura, Lindsay Stein and Chris Daniels. 2015. 'Waging War Against Extremists on the Internet'. *PR Week*, www.prweek.com/article/1335178/waging-war-against-extremists-internet (accessed 21 September 2017).

North Atlantic Treaty Organization. 2016. *Cyber Defence Pledge*, www.nato.int/cps/en/ natohq/official_texts_133177.htm (accessed 23 October 2017).

O'Connor, Alan. 2004. 'Punk and Globalization: Spain and Mexico'. *International Journal of Cultural Studies*, 7(2), pp. 175–195.

Olofinbiyi, Sogo Angel and Jean Steyn. 2018. 'The Boko Haram Terrorism: Causes Still Misunderstood'. *Journal of Social Sciences*, 14, pp. 129–144.

'Operation Ice ISIS: "Anonymous" Hackers Take on Extremist Group on Social Media'. 2014. *Informed Comment*, www.juancole.com/2014/09/operation-anonymous-extremist. html (accessed 18 September 2017).

Osborne, Samuel. 2015. 'ISIS Has Started Recruiting in China With a Song in Mandarin'. *Independent*, www.independent.co.uk/news/world/asia/isis-has-started-recruiting-in-china-with-a-song-in-mandarin-a6766721.html (accessed 26 March 2019).

Oster, Erik. 2018. 'Ogilvy Survey Shows Trust in Traditional Media Is Continuing to Erode'. *AdWeek*, www.adweek.com/digital/ogilvy-survey-shows-trust-in-traditional-media-is-continuing-to-erode/ (accessed 25 March 2019).

Parmelee, John and Shannon Bichard. 2012. *Politics and the Twitter Revolution*. Lanham: Lexington Books.

Patel, Faiza. 2015. 'Why the Social Media Giants Can't Ever Wipe Out ISIS Propaganda'. *Brennan Center For Justice*, www.brennancenter.org/analysis/why-social-media-giants-cant-ever-wipe-out-isis-propaganda (accessed 20 September 2017).

Paul, Katie. 2014. 'Résumé of a 21st Century Terrorist: The Social Media and Marketing Major'. *Anthropaulicy*, http://anthropaulicy.blogspot.co.uk/2014/06/resume-of-21st-century-terrorist-social.html (accessed 18 September 2017).

Pavlik, John V. 1996. *Social and Cultural Consequences in New Media Technology: Cultural and Commercial Perspectives*. Boston: Pearson Allyn and Bacon.

Pellerin, Clara. 2016. 'Communicating Terror: An Analysis of ISIS Communication Strategy'. *Sciences Po*, https://www.sciencespo.fr/.../KSP_Paper_Award_Spring_2016_PELLERIN_Clara.pdf (accessed 18 June 2019).

Perez, Evan and Shimon Prokupecz. 2015. 'Paris Attackers Likely Used Encrypted Apps, Officials Say'. *CNN*, http://edition.cnn.com/2015/12/17/politics/paris-attacks-terrorists-encryption/index.html (accessed 19 July 2017).

Petersen, Kim. 2015. 'In the Fight for Peace and Social Justice Is Mass Media or Anonymous the Answer?'. *Dissidentvoice.org*, http://dissidentvoice.org/2015/11/in-the-fight-for-peace-and-social-justice-is-mass-media-or-anonymous-the-answer/ (accessed 18 September 2017).

Philps, Alan. 2015. 'Interview: Farah Pandith'. *The World Today*, 71(2), www.chathamhouse.org/publication/interview-farah-pandith (accessed 10 January 2018).

Phyrillas, Tony. 2015. 'Rep: Joe Pitts: Social Media Is a New Front in War on Terror'. *Tony Phyrillas*, http://tonyphyrillas.blogspot.co.uk/2015/12/rep-joe-pitts-social-media-is-new-front.html (accessed 19 September 2017).

Picazo-Vela, Sergio, ISIS Gutiérrez-Martínez and Luis Felipe Luna-Reyes. 2012. 'Understanding Risks, Benefits, and Strategic Alternatives of Social Media Applications in the Public Sector'. *Government Information Quarterly*, 29, pp. 504–511.

'PM Announces £5 Million For Commonwealth Counter-Extremism Unit'. 2015. *UK Government*, www.gov.uk/government/news/pm-announces-5-million-for-commonwealth-counter-extremism-unit (accessed 21 September 2017).

Powell, Adam. 2015. 'Google Policy Director: "ISIS Is Having a Viral Moment on Social Media and the Countervailing Viewpoints Are Nowhere Near Strong Enough to Oppose Them"'. *The Public Diplomacy Council*, www.publicdiplomacycouncil.org/commentaries/07-26-15/google-policy-director-%E2%80%9Cisis-having-viral-moment-social-media-and-countervaili (accessed 18 September 2017).

Power, Brad. 2015. *The Virtual Caliphate: The Behind-The-Scenes Bloody Propaganda Strategy*. North Charleston: CreateSpace Independent Publishing.

Power, Samantha. 2015. 'Putting ISIS Out of Business'. *CNN*, https://edition.cnn.com/2015/12/17/opinions/samantha-power-putting-isis-out-of-business/index.html (accessed 4 January 2019).

'Reaching Maturity in Government Use of Social Media'. 2015. *OECD Insights Blog*, http://oecdinsights.org/2015/08/21/reaching-maturity-in-government-use-of-social-media/ (accessed 21 September 2017).

Reitman, Janet. 2015. 'The Children of ISIS'. *Rolling Stone*, www.rollingstone.com/culture/features/teenage-jihad-inside-the-world-of-american-kids-seduced-by-isis-2015 0325 (accessed 25 April 2017).

Reuters. 2016. 'Twitter Shuts Down 360,000 Accounts for Links to Terrorism'. *Newsweek*, www.newsweek.com/twitter-islamic-state-360000-isis-accounts-terrorism-al-qaeda-491568 (accessed 21 September 2017).

Reuters. 2017. 'Britain, France to Join Forces to Combat Online Extremism – May'. *CNBC*, www.cnbc.com/2017/06/13/britain-france-to-join-forces-to-combat-online-extremism–may.html (accessed 17 September 2017).

Reuters in New York. 2015. 'Security Council Unanimously Calls on UN Members to Fight ISIS'. *The Guardian*, www.theguardian.com/world/2015/nov/21/un-calls-for-all-able-member-states-to-join-fight-against-isis (accessed 10 September 2017).

Richards, Barry. 2004. 'Terrorism and Public Relations'. *Public Relations Review*, 30, pp. 169–176.

Richards, Barry. 2007. *Emotional Governance Politics, Media and Terror*. Basingstoke: Palgrave Macmillan.

Richards, Imogen. 2016. '"Flexible" Capital Accumulation in Islamic State Social Media'. *Critical Studies on Terrorism*, 9, pp. 205–225.

Ritholtz, Barry. 2015. 'A Year of Islamic State Terror'. *The Big Picture*, http://ritholtz.com/2015/11/a-year-of-islamic-state-terror/ (accessed 18 September 2017).

Roberts, Craig S. 2012. *Applied Evolutionary Psychology*. New York: Oxford University Press.

Rogers, Paul. 2016. *Irregular War: ISIS and the New Threat From the Margins*. London: IB Tauris.

Ross, Alec. 2017. 'The Revolution Will Be Tweeted'. *Friends & Family – A Narrative History of Diplomacy*, www.bbc.co.uk/programmes/b08drjdx (accessed 11 March 2017).

Rozumski, Paul K. 2015. *Evolution of Cyber Technologies and Operations to 2035 – Chapter: The Rise of Social Media and Its Role in Future Protests and Revolutions*. Switzerland: Springer International Publishing.

'Russia's Zuckerberg Launches Telegram, a New Instant Messenger Service'. 2013. *Reuters*, www.reuters.com/article/idUS74722569420130830 (accessed 4 March 2017).

Rutter, Tamsin. 2014. 'Why People Are Not Engaged in Politics and Policymaking – And How to Fix It'. *The Guardian*, www.theguardian.com/public-leaders-network/2014/apr/01/david-blunkett-involving-people-politics-policymaking (accessed 25 March 2019).

Said, Edward W. 2003. *Orientalism*. London: Penguin Books.

Saif, Hassan, Miriam Fernandez, Matthew Rowe and Harith Alani. 2016. *On the Role of Semantics for Detecting Pro-ISIS Stances on Social Media*. London: The Open University.

Sanchez, Dr Justin. 2016. 'Narrative Networks'. *Defense Advanced Research Projects Agency*, www.darpa.mil/program/narrative-networks (accessed 21 September 2017).

Sandre, Andreas. 2015. *Digital Diplomacy: Conversations on Innovation in Foreign Policy*. Lanham: Rowman & Littlefield Publishers.

Sartre, Jean-Paul. 2003. *Being and Nothingness: An Essay on Phenomenological Ontology*. London: Routledge.

Saunders, Andrew. 2016. 'What's an Ex-British Diplomat Doing Heading Tata in Europe?'. *Management Today*, www.managementtoday.co.uk/whats-ex-british-diplomat-doing-heading-tata-europe/article/1360692 (accessed 26 March 2019).

Scarr, Lanai and Armando Cordoba. 2015. 'More Australians Joining ISIS With 30 Deaths Confirmed'. *News Corp Australia*, www.news.com.au/national/more-australians-joining-isis-with-30-deaths-confirmed/story-fncynjr2-1227308688607 (accessed 26 March 2019).

Schmidt, Eric and Jared Cohen. 2013. *The New Digital Age – Reshaping the Future of People, Nations and Business*. London: John Murray.

Schneider, Nathan K. 2015. 'ISIS and Social Media: The Combatant Commander's Guide to Countering ISIS's Social Media Campaign'. *Defence Technical Information Centre, Naval War College Newport – Joint Military Operations Dept.*, www.dtic.mil/docs/citations/ADA621060 (accessed 12 April 2017).

Schwarzwalder, Rob. 2015. 'ISIS Isn't About Jobs'. *Canon and Culture*, www.canonandculture.com/isis-isnt-about-jobs/ (accessed 18 September 2017).

Seip, Mark. 2016. *Harnessing Communications and Public Diplomacy: Four Rules for Success in Strategic Development*. Washington, DC: Atlantic Council.

Shaw, Adrian. 2007. 'Terror Videos Found At 21/7 Homes'. *Daily Mirror*, www.mirror.co.uk/news/uk-news/terror-videos-found-at-217-homes-451936 (accessed 21 September 2017).

Shiloach, Gilad. 2014. 'Crowdsourcing Terror: ISIS Asks for Ideas on Killing Jordanian Pilot'. *Vocativ*, www.vocativ.com/world/isis-2/suggestions-kill-pilot/ (accessed 21 September 2017).

Sir Jenkins, John. 2016. 'University of Buckingham Evening Seminar'. MA International Affairs and Diplomacy (by Research).

Slavin, Barbara. 2015. 'Islamic State Brutality Could Backfire'. *Small Wars Journal*, http://smallwarsjournal.com/blog/islamic-state-brutality-could-backfire (accessed 19 September 2017).

Smith, Laura. 2017. 'Messaging App Telegram Centrepiece of IS Social Media Strategy'. *BBC News*, www.bbc.co.uk/news/technology-39743252 (accessed 29 June 2017).

Solomon, Hussein. 2016. 'Accounting for Islamic State's Appeal and Resilience'. In *Islamic State and the Coming Global Confrontation*. Cham: Springer International Publishing.

Sparre, Kirsten. 2001. 'Megaphone Diplomacy in the Northern Irish Peace Process: Squaring the Circle by Talking to Terrorists Through Journalists'. *The Harvard International Journal of Press/Politics*, 6, pp. 88–104.

Speckhard, Anne and Ahmet S. Yayla. 2016a. *ISIS Defectors: Inside Stories of the Terrorist Caliphate*. McLean: Advances Press.

Speckhard, Anne and Ahmet S. Yayla. 2016b. 'American ISIS Defector Mohamad Jamal Khweis & the Threat Posed By "Clean Skin" Terrorists: Unanswered Questions and Confirmations'. *ICSVE*, www.icsve.org/brief-reports/american-isis-defector/ (accessed 25 November 2018).

Speckhard, Anne and Ahmet S. Yayla. 2017. 'Telegram: The Mighty Application that ISIS Loves'. *ICSVE*, www.icsve.org/brief-reports/telegram-the-mighty-application-that-isis-loves/ (accessed 10 July 2017).

Spencer, Robert. 2015. *The Complete Infidel's Guide to ISIS*. Washington, DC: Regnery Publishing.

'Spring 2015 Survey'. 2015. *Pew Research Center's Global Attitudes Project*, www.pewglobal.org/2015/06/23/spring-2015-survey/ (accessed 21 September 2017).

'Srdja Popovic'. 2019. *Harvard Kennedy School*, www.hks.harvard.edu/faculty/srdja-popovic (accessed 25 March 2019).

Steadman, Ian. 2014. 'Why Terrorists Tweet About Cats'. *New Statesman*, www.newstatesman.com/world-affairs/2014/06/why-terrorists-tweet-about-cats (accessed 12 January 2019).

Steed, Brian L. 2016. *ISIS: An Introduction and Guide to the Islamic State*. Santa Barbara, CA: ABC-CLIO.

Stern, Jessica. 2015. 'Obama and Terrorism'. *Foreign Affairs*, pp. 62–70.

Stern, Jessica and J. M. Berger. 2015. *ISIS: The State of Terror*. London: William Collins, pp. 36–38, 145–147.

Stewart, Heather. 2017. 'May Calls on Internet Firms to Remove Extremist Content Within Two Hours'. *The Guardian*, www.theguardian.com/uk-news/2017/sep/19/theresa-may-will-tell-internet-firms-to-tackle-extremist-content (accessed 20 September 2017).

Stuster, Dana J. 2013. '9 Disturbingly Good Jihadi Raps'. *Foreign Policy*, http://foreign policy.com/2013/04/29/9-disturbingly-good-jihadi-raps/ (accessed 21 September 2017).

'Terrorist Social Media Cases Test Scope of CDA § 230'. 2016. *Cyber Report*, https://ilccyberreport.wordpress.com/2016/07/13/terrorist-social-media-cases-test-scope-of-cda-%C2%A7-230/ (accessed 19 September 2017).

Thames, Knox. 2014. 'Opportunities to Combat Violent Religious Extremism'. *Small Wars Journal*, https://smallwarsjournal.com/index.php/jrnl/art/opportunities-to-combat-violent-religious-extremism (accessed 26 March 2019).

Tharoor, Kanishk. 2015. 'The Spectacle of Solidarity'. *The Hindu Business Line*, www.thehindubusinessline.com/blink/talk/the-spectacle-of-solidarity/article7899699.ece (accessed 16 July 2017).

Thompson, Lauren. 2015. 'No Safe Spaces: Missouri, ISIS, and What We Can Do About It'. *Nursing Clio*, https://nursingclio.org/2015/12/01/no-safe-spaces-missouri-isis-and-what-we-can-do-about-it/ (accessed 18 January 2018).

Timreck, Sarah. 2017. 'Winning Hearts and Minds From ISIS'. *Peacefare.Net*, www.peacefare.net/2017/01/27/winning-the-hearts-and-minds-campaign-against-isis/ (accessed 18 September 2018).

Travis, Alan. 2017. 'Britain Has Large Audience for Online Jihadist Propaganda, Report Says'. *The Guardian*, www.theguardian.com/world/2017/sep/19/britain-has-large-audience-for-online-jihadist-propaganda-report-says (accessed 19 September 2018).

'Trump's Twitter Year of Outrage and Braggadocio'. 2018. *Politico*, www.politico.com/interactives/2018/interactive_donald-trump-twitter-2018-analysis/ (accessed 25 March 2019).

Trussler, Marc and Stuart Soroka. 'Consumer Demand for Cynical and Negative News Frames'. *The International Journal of Press/Politics*, 19(3), pp. 360–379.

Turley, Jonathan. 2014. 'The Faces of ISIS Facebook: Australian Boy and English Rapper Pose with Severed Heads on Islamic State Social Media'. *Jonanthanturley.org*, https://jonanthanturley.org/2014/08/14/the-faces-of-isis-facebook-australian-boy-and-english-rapper-pose-with-severed-heads-on-islamic-state-social-media/ (accessed 19 September 2017).

'Twiplomacy Study 2018'. 2018. *Twiplomacy*, https://twiplomacy.com/blog/twiplomacy-study-2018/ (accessed 25 March 2019).

Tzu, Sun. 2014. *The Art of War*. London: Arcturus.

Ubayasiri, Kasun. 2004. 'Virtual Hostage Dramas and Real Politics'. *Ejournalist*, http://acquire.cqu.edu.au:8080/vital/access/manager/Repository/cqu:1302 (accessed 4 December 2018).

UK Communications Committee. 2012. 'Chapter 2: The Economic Challenge'. *UK Parliament*, https://publications.parliament.uk/pa/ld201012/ldselect/ldcomuni/256/25605.htm (accessed 21 September 2018).

UK Foreign and Commonwealth Office. 2016. 'Social Media Use'. *Gov.uk* www.gov.uk/government/organisations/foreign-commonwealth-office/about/social-media-use (accessed 21 September 2018).

UK Government. 2017. *Cyber and Security Government Directorate*, www.gov.uk/government/groups/office-of-cyber-security-and-information-assurance (accessed 21 October 2018).

'Unfriended'. 2015. *The Economist*, p. 11.

'UN Human Rights Panel Concludes ISIL Is Committing Genocide Against Yazidis'. 2016. *UN News Center*, www.un.org/apps/news/story.asp?NewsID=54247 (accessed 18 October 2018).

United Nations Office on Drugs and Crime. 2012. *The Use of the Internet for Terrorism Purposes*. Vienna: Publishing and Library Section, United Nations Office at Vienna.

U.S. Customs and Border Protection. 2019. 'Official ESTA Application'. *Department of Homeland Security*, https://esta.cbp.dhs.gov/esta/ (accessed 26 March 2019).

U.S. Department of State. 2017. *Bureau of Counterterrorism and Countering Violent Extremism*, www.state.gov/j/ct/ (accessed 23 October 2018).

US Navy. 2015. 'Latest Info for Sailors and Families on ISIS List'. *Navy Live*, http://navylive.dodlive.mil/2015/03/26/latest-info-for-sailors-and-families-on-isis-list/ (accessed 20 September 2018).

Van Buren, Peter. 2016. 'We're Winning the War Against ISIS! Maybe? On Social Media?'. *Anti-War Blog*, www.antiwar.com/blog/2016/09/22/were-winning-the-war-against-isis-maybe-on-social-media/ (accessed 19 September 2017).

Waddington, Stephen. 2017. 'Making Sense of Mary Meeker's Internet Trends Report'. *Ketchum.com*, www.ketchum.com/making-sense-mary-meeker%E2%80%99s-internet-trends-report (accessed 4 July 2017).

Walker, Lauren. 2015. 'The War Against ISIS . . . Online'. *Newsweek Global*, 164, pp. 20–21.

Wanlund, Bill. 2015. 'Intelligence Reform: Are U.S. Spy Agencies Prepared for 21St-Century Threats?'. *CQ Press*, http://library.cqpress.com/cqresearcher/document.php?id=cqresrre2015052900 (accessed 18 September 2017).

Washington DC, Treasury Department. 2016. 'Remarks By the President After Counter-ISIL Meeting'. *Whitehouse.gov*, https://obamawhitehouse.archives.gov/the-press-office/2016/06/14/remarks-president-after-counter-isil-meeting (accessed 7 June 2017).

'Weapons of ISIS – Islamic State Infantry Weapons, Vehicles and Artillery'. 2019. *Military Factory*, www.militaryfactory.com/smallarms/weapons-of-isis.asp (accessed 26 March 2019).

Weimann, Gabriel. 2016. *The Emerging Role of Social Media in the Recruitment of Foreign Fighters, In: Foreign Fighters Under International Law and Beyond*. The Hague: TMC Asser Press.

Weiss, Michael and Hassan Hassan. 2015. *ISIS: Inside the Army of Terror*. New York: Regan Arts.

West, Lindsay A., Richard V. Martin, Courtney Perkins, Jennifer M. Quatel and Gavin Macgregor-Skinner. 2016. 'Opposing Viewpoints on Youth Social Media Banning in the U.S. for the Combatance of Extremist Recruiting'. *International Journal of Cyber Warfare and Terrorism*, 6, pp. 1–12.

'Why ISIS Is Winning the Social Media War'. 2016. *Wired*, www.wired.com/2016/03/isis-winning-social-media-war-heres-beat/ (accessed 19 September 2018).

Williams, Lauren. 2016. 'Islamic State Propaganda and the Mainstream Media'. *Lowy Institute*, www.lowyinstitute.org/sites/default/files/islamic-state-propaganda-western-media_0.pdf (accessed 8 May 2018).

Willnat, Lars and David H. Weaver. 2018. 'Social Media and U.S. Journalists'. *Digital Journalism*, 6(7), pp. 889–909.

Wilts, Alexandra. 2017. 'Trump to Scrap "Muslim Ban" and Replace It With New Targeted Restrictions, Says Official'. *The Independent*, www.independent.co.uk/news/world/americas/us-politics/trump-muslim-ban-scrap-restrictions-travel-countries-list-reports-a7961956.html (accessed 22 September 2018).

Winter, Charlie. 2015. 'Documenting the Virtual "Caliphate"'. *Quilliam*, www.quilliaminternational.com/wp-content/uploads/2015/10/FINAL-documenting-the-virtual-caliphate.pdf (accessed 21 September 2018).

Withnall, Adam. 2014. 'ISIS Releases "Abhorrent" Sex Slaves Pamphlet With 27 Tips for Militants on Taking, Punishing and Raping Female Captives'. *The Independent*, www.independent.co.uk/news/world/middle-east/isis-releases-abhorrent-sex-slaves-pamphlet-with-27-tips-for-militants-on-taking-punishing-and-9915913.html (accessed 21 September 2017).

Wittes, Benjamin. 2017. 'Another Day, Another Material Support Suit Against a Social Media Company'. *Lawfare*, www.lawfareblog.com/another-day-another-material-support-suit-against-social-media-company (accessed 20 September 2018).

'Wondering How You Go About Joining ISIS?'. 2019. *Open Your Eyes*, https://openyoureyes.net/category/joining-isis/ (accessed 26 March 2019).

Wood, Graeme. 2015. 'What ISIS Really Wants'. *The Atlantic*, https://www.theatlantic.com/magazine/archive/2015/03/what-isis-really-wants/384980/ (accessed 18 June 2019).

Woolf, Nicky. 2016. 'Obama Is Worried About Fake News on Social Media'. *The Guardian*, www.theguardian.com/media/2016/nov/20/barack-obama-facebook-fake-news-problem (accessed 20 September 2017).

Yergin, Daniel. 2009. *The Prize: The Epic Quest for Oil, Money & Power*. London: Simon & Schuster, 536 pp.

Zenko, Micah. 2015. 'The National Commission on the War on Terrorism Is Hereby Called to Order'. *Foreign Policy*, https://foreignpolicy.com/2015/06/30/the-national-commission-on-the-war-on-terrorism-is-hereby-called-to-order-counterterrorism-strategy/ (accessed 25 March 2019).

Zimbardo, Philip G. 2004. 'A Situationist Perspective on the Psychology of Evil: Understanding How Good People Are Transformed Into Perpetrators'. In *The Social Psychology of Good and Evil*. A. G. Miller (ed.). New York: The Guilford Press, pp. 21–50.

INDEX